THE EXECUTION OF
JESUS CHRIST

THE EXECUTION OF JESUS CHRIST

Touching the fellowship of his suffering and experiencing the power of his resurrection…

Adam LiVecchi

All scripture taken from the King James Version which is in the Public Domain.

THE EXECUTION OF JESUS CHRIST

ISBN 978-0-9835523-1-4

© 2011 by Adam LiVecchi. All Rights Reserved. This book is protected by the copyright laws of The United States of America. No part of this publication may be reproduced, stored in a retrieval system, or transmitted, in any form or by any means, electronic, mechanical, photocopying, recording, or otherwise, without the prior written permission of the publisher, or under consentual agreement.

Printed in the United States of America.

First Printing: May 2011

For more information on how to order this book or any of the other materials that We See Jesus Ministries offers, please contact:

We See Jesus Ministries
www.WeSeeJesusMinistries.com

Dedication

This book is dedicated to Jesus Christ, the lamb that was slain from before the foundation of the world. Jesus you are still my very best friend. I love spending time with you more than anything else in this life. Thank you for rescuing my life and family. You have been faithful to your word please help me to be faithful to mine.

Special thanks to -

My beloved Sarah - you are an amazing wife. You are the most encouraging, helpful, loving, patient person I have ever met. Your words of encouragement have pushed me forward in every aspect of life. I love you Sarah.

My brother Aaron - I am so proud of you. It is amazing that we get to travel together and minister Christ to the world, as well as the church. You are faithful, and loyal. The ministry that comes from you is not fashioned after man or a model but after your time with Jesus. Stay strong and don't go with the flow.

My Father and Mother - Thank you for laying down your life, thank you for not giving up, thank you for fighting the good fight of faith.

A very special thank you to the We See Jesus Ministries board as well as Steve and Christina Stewart of Impact Nations, you are amazing spiritual parents. I love and honor you for living a crucified life by serving the poor of the earth with selfless and fearless love. You guys are living the Kingdom so many speak about. You are heroes to me.

Also a very special thanks you to Dr. Sandy Kirk for your patience with me. Thank you for preaching the purest gospel I have ever heard. Let the preaching of Christ and him crucified cause the nations to tremble and the Father to smile.

Contents

Chapter 1
    Take up your Cross and Follow me   9

Chapter 2
    The stretching of the cross   15

Chapter 3
    The thorns, nails and the piercing   21

Chapter 4
    The fellowship of his sufferings   31

Chapter 5
    The measurements of love   43

Chapter 6
    When darkness covered all the earth   49

Chapter 7
    Jesus speaks from the cross   53

Chapter 8
    The Five Wise Virgins   59

Chapter 9
    The offense of the cross   69

Chapter 10
    The marks of the cross   77

Chapter 11
    When we can no longer carry our cross   83

Chapter 12
    The prayer of the cross   91

Chapter 13
    Arise and shine   99

Chapter 14
    The centrality of true outpouring   105

Chapter 15
    Living in the reward of His suffering   115

Chapter 16
    The soon coming tension
    and the righteous judgments of God   123

Chapter 17
    They that are Christ's   127

Chapter 18
    None should perish   131

Chapter 1
Take up your cross and follow me

God is so kind. He would never tell us to do something He wouldn't do Himself. Jesus is the kindest person I have ever known, the more I get to know Jesus the more I see how humble and patient he is, and the more my heart expands. The more our hearts expand the larger Jesus becomes in us. In three of the glorious Gospels we have a very similar verse. It is found in Matthew 16:24, Mark 8:34, and Luke 9:23. I will use Luke 9:23 for our reading together *"And he said to them all, If any man will come after me, let him deny himself and take up his cross daily, and follow me."* There are conditions if we want to follow Jesus, we cannot serve God on our own terms. In the Old Testament, and the High Priest would have a rope tied to his foot, in case he wanted to serve God on his own terms. In the Book of Acts chapter 5, Ananias and Sapphira wanted to serve God on their own terms and they left Peter's Revival service in a body bag. The Kingdom of God is not Burger King, and you can never have it your way. It is Jesus' way or no way or we are just plain lost.

Before we can follow Jesus really, we must deny ourselves or utterly deny ourselves. Meaning we must literally disown ourselves. If we disown ourselves and become the property of the one who bought us with His precious Blood then we are no longer thieves trying to steal our own life back from Jesus who paid for it. Then we are ready to begin to follow the Lamb of God, wherever he will go. In Matthew 10 Jesus says many interesting things, He talks of those who are worthy of Him. Only carrying a cross makes you worthy of him. When Jesus, a Jewish itinerant minister, tells his disciples to take up their cross and follow him, he is making a profound statement. In our culture, it would be like "take up your electric chair and follow me to freedom and life everlasting." The cross was a pagan instrument of death, which was pretty successful in killing anyone who was put on it! "Hey Jesus, I thought you came to rule and deliver, what about the whole abundant life thing?" Jesus is asking his followers to deny themselves and to follow him. Crosses were heavy, "Jesus, you said your yoke was easy and your burden is light". They must have been stunned when he said, *"Deny yourself, take up your cross and follow me."* The cultural shock value to the Jewish people on this was off the charts. In Matthew 9, Jesus was healing the sick and raising the dead. Then he had a compassion based Prayer meeting where his disciples became the answer to their own Prayers, and where he later sent them out to preach the Kingdom and Heal the Sick. Before Jesus the Lord of the Harvest sent forth his laborers to heal, He told them how to become worthy of him by carrying a pagan instrument of death and following him. My question would have been, "how are we going to heal people while carrying a pagan instrument of death and by the way, where are we going?" Sometimes as we read the gospel we forget Jesus is talking to real people, with real emotions and real problems.

The natural man cannot even begin to understand the things of the Spirit. Some of the things that Jesus says in Scripture just totally blow me away; my heart becomes so fascinated when Jesus says things like this. How did his disciples feel? What were their thoughts? He was just raising the dead, and now he is asking them to carry a pagan instrument of death and go and heal people? No Jewish man would want to carry a pagan instrument of death, pagans or heathens were considered to be unclean, Peter didn't even want to eat what they ate and this is even after Pentecost. The cross was a heavy, painful, and slow instrument of death. For anyone to carry such a thing would be against his or her free will.

Anything that is against what we want is self-denial, which is what God loves, because then we can begin to carry our cross and follow his Son. God's will is that we surrender our will fully to him. Those who are searching for God's will, will not find it if they are not surrendering their will. Jesus said to deny yourself, God wouldn't tell you to do something he wouldn't do. Jesus was God's flesh; He was God in the flesh. He was recognized by Elizabeth, John the Baptist's mother, as Lord even when he was in the womb. Fully God fully man, perfect flesh, sinless, blameless, spotless and Holy, undefiled, manifested for sacrifice only! In Mark 15: 34 we hear the Cry of Dereliction. *"And in the ninth hour Jesus cried with a loud voice, saying, Eloi, Eloi, lama sabach' thani? Which is being interpreted, My God, My God why hast thou forsaken me?"* God denied himself, so in turn we have to. Jesus is just as much a part of the Triune God head as Holy Spirit or the Father Himself. God denied his flesh so that we could be reconciled to God. Therefore we need to deny our flesh so we can follow the one who shed His very own Blood for us. It is a must; there is no other way. What really is interesting to me is that all three of the Glorious Gospels have the account of "take up your cross". However, it is not found in the Gospel of John, but John is found at the Cross of Christ. John's dedication to the cross and to following Jesus probably had a vast part to due with why He received the Revelation of Jesus Christ, the last book of the Bible. To John, Jesus revealed himself as a Lamb. One day the earth will want to hide from this lamb. This same Lamb, that bore the Wrath of God, will pour out that same Wrath for those who deny his right to purchase them by his precious Blood. The Blood of the Lamb that was over the doorposts in Egypt covered only those who were in the house. They had to be inside on his terms. Therefore we must be in him, inside his Holy Word, and it has to be his way! Just three feet outside of the house the Blood would have no affect, it must be his way for he is the Way and how he does things reveals who he is. The ways of God reveal the nature of God, the same way the words of a person reveal what is really inside that person.

His ways are unsearchable and high above our ways, we should learn to walk in them, and his plan is a lot better for us than we think.

The weight of the Cross is supposed to cripple our carnal man, similar to Jacob wrestling with the Angel until He walked with a limp and had his named changed, and became Blessed. One of the greatest blessings from God is to have a deep revelation of "not to put any confidence in the flesh." Maybe with a limp Jacob realized this. Remember everyone in the kingdom walks with a limp, he who has ears to hear let them hear. Carrying the Cross is something that will take all of our effort and some grace. We cannot have mixed interests carrying a cross; all we can do is carry a cross. During the time we carry the cross it is then when we count the cost deeply and the reality of painful slow death really grabs a hold of us in a terrifying way. Every one of Jesus' disciples dropped their cross when Jesus had to carry his and get on it. Only John the beloved revelator went back to the cross, which could be why he had so much Revelation. There is a special blessing for just reading the Book of Revelation. *Being with others in their darkest hours is part of the test to see if you can be trusted with the Light of Revelation.* Counting the cost is a part of carrying the cross. Jesus isn't looking for some emotional decision during a good song on Sunday morning; although it may start there it will definitely not end there. The cross is meant to kill, and it's God's agenda to get rid of our old life so he can give us Eternal New life in His Precious Son.

The cross is meant to kill the stuff in us that will later kill us, if not dealt with. Remember if we don't deal with our issues, our issues will deal with us. One day the Holy Spirit whispered something marvelous to me. He said, *"There is no way that you can carry a cross and not be marked by it."* I love when the Holy Spirit speaks. Jesus seems to be his favorite topic, maybe because Jesus never grieved or quenched him, who knows! Holy Spirit loves to speak of the things Jesus has suffered for us, our worth is found in the price Christ paid for us not in what we do, or accomplish in ministry or in how much we pray and fast. Many people have no idea of their value so they spend themselves on things that are worthless because they feel worthless. This is a result of the Cross not really being preached with revelation or passion for the Son of God. I have friends who are different cultures not just American, and I have realized that the same problem arises in other cultures. The cross is hardly preached, many want Pentecost with no Crucifixion and it simply will never happen. *The preaching of the cross is the Wisdom of God.* Everything must be built upon Wisdom. Wisdom has seven pillars, which are also the seven Spirits of God spoken of in Revelation 4:5 and Revelation 5:6. The preaching of the cross is what establishes wisdom's house.

When Jesus was on the way to Jerusalem in Mark chapter 10, he began to tell His disciples the things he would suffer. He actually prophesied the order of his own sufferings. *Mark 10:33-35 "Saying Behold, we go to Jerusalem; and the Son of Man shall be delivered unto the Chief Priests, and unto the Scribes; and shall be delivered to the Gentiles: And they shall mock him and shall scourge him, and shall spit upon him, and shall kill him: and the third day he shall rise again. And James and John the sons of Zebedee come unto him, saying Master we would that you should do for us whatsoever we shall desire."* Jesus is telling his closest friends the deepest and most intimate thing, the very reason he became flesh and came to the earth. Here he is telling them his purpose. Unfortunately they had no interest in what he was saying, they only had interest in what he could do for them. They were very sincere in their request but they were sincerely wrong. They desired Isaiah 63 before Isaiah 53, but God does things in order. I was reading this verse and I began to weep and say Precious Jesus, forgive me. These are symptoms of betrayal, this is the exact opposite of *"deny yourself and take up your cross"*, and we as a people are so self-absorbed it is gross. The cross is the only way God will deal with us. The death of the cross releases the power of resurrection to overcome self.

Jesus was prophesying about his soon coming destiny, and they didn't want to hear it on their prophetic journey to Jerusalem. Instead they were having delusions of grandeur about a throne, and who was the greatest. They were speaking to Jesus like he is a genie in a bottle, this is like very many of the prayer meetings that go on today. There is a shift coming in prayer, after men meet Jesus on the cross they will know how to pray. Jesus even prayed on the cross, that's how essential the prayer of the cross is. What is interesting is God the Father answered his prayer. The cross is even the answer to prayer. All prayer from the cross is heard. Prayer that is heard from the cross is not selfish prayer, but *"Father forgive them for they know not what they do."* And so while we are on the cross and our life is slowly leaking out, self tends to be silent when it is God who led us to the cross and not our own foolish actions. Many immature Christians call paying for their foolish actions, carrying their cross. This is not true; they are only reaping what they have sowed. *The cross is not a penalty but a privilege.* It takes spiritual discernment and understanding to perceive the roots of our suffering in this life. Some suffering has to do with our right actions or words, some suffering is just simply because we belong to Jesus. Other suffering is simply the fruit of foolish choices. I fully trust the Holy Spirit to give us discernment in these circumstances, so we can walk in wisdom and avoid any unnecessary trouble in this life.

Chapter 2
The stretching of the cross

Song of Solomon 7:10 "I am my beloved's and his desire is toward me"

This is a Bride's understanding of her Bridegroom's emotions or passion for her. The word "desire" literally means longing and stretching out. The topic of Jesus being stretched out is not really spoken about much. Neither is the cross, but it was during his Crucifixion where he was stretched out. In the Song of Solomon there are a few more verses that touch the point of a Bride understanding that a Bridegroom has purchased her; this is an important Truth that will be more widely understood as Jesus apprehends a Bridal company in this hour. Jesus body was stretched to the max. If you held a balloon full of water and I pulled on it until the balloon popped and the water spilled out that would be a word picture of what happened to Jesus physical body on the cross. There is a mystery involved in the stretching that happened to the body of Christ while he was on the cross. *Psalm 22:14 "I am poured out like water, and all my bones are out of joint: My heart is like wax; it is melted in the midst of my bowels."* The Hebrew word for "out of joint" literally means stretch and to be out of joint. Jesus was stretched to the point where literally every bone was out of place and not one bone was broken. How does that happen so perfectly? This is a matter of God's Sovereignty, and also a fulfillment of prophecy that not one of his bones shall be broken found in Psalm 34:20 and John 19:36. What is interesting about Prophecy is it is in part but fulfilled in whole. When something is prophesied in Scripture and then later fulfilled in Scripture there is much to learn in the time of the prophecy and the setting and how and if more happened when the fulfillment of the word came to pass. For example, the Holy Spirit revealed that Simeon would see the Lord's Christ before he died, but Scripture does not tell us that He would hold Jesus and Prophesy to Mary, see Luke 2:26-35.

Even Jesus' death was Miraculous! The custom in Rome was to break the legs of men who were crucified so that they would suffocate. Yet Jesus said, no man takes my life, I lay it down. Jesus offered his breathe to his Father, so that when the Romans came to him they did not break his legs yet they pierced His side to fulfill the prophecy in Zechariah (Zechariah 13:1). One of Jesus' names from Isaiah chapter 9 is "wonderful" which literally means a "miracle." If you don't believe in miracles then you don't believe in Jesus. If you don't expect miracles then you don't expect the Lord Jesus to break in on your situation. If this is you, you need to sit at his feet and hear his word to break that spirit of unbelief off of you. Unbelief is like quick sand! Jesus' heart was ruptured for us and he is touched with our infirmities, the stretching that happened to his body happens to us in the Spirit. We need a broken heart to serve God his way, and serving God will break our heart. The cross is where the hearts of men are broken. Jesus' heart was moved with compassion, so much so that it melted like wax and it literally was fully poured out on the cross. Seeing the poor could make you feel compassion that can be stirred up by the soul of man and only be temporary. Worldly people and false religions feed the poor, give medical aid and the whole nine yards. All of those actions are good or from the knowledge of the Tree of good and evil, but it is not Holy Spirit. The broken heart that the cross makes manifest is spiritual and cannot be worked up by the soul. I am involved in missions work and I love the poor. For what we do to the poor we are actually doing to Jesus. God may use the poor to break your heart or deeply touch your feelings, *but what Jesus did on the cross is God's main instrument of breaking your heart.* After we die on the cross we are a partaker of the Tree of Life, spiritually those who overcome will literally eat from the Tree of Life that is in Heaven. It is probably the same tree that was in the Garden before the garden was closed to men (this is just a thought please don't put me on a heresy website). Now redeemed, hearts of blood bought men and women are the garden that finds pleasure in the Son of God forevermore.

Only the cross produces a broken heart and a contrite spirit, which is something that the Father will not despise for it pleased him to bruise Jesus (Isaiah 53). The wrath of God was satisfied in Jesus. The only ones who will receive Wrath from the Lamb are those who didn't accept his sacrifice. The Hebrew word for bruise means to crumble, contrite, crush, beat to pieces or humble. That is what happened to Jesus for us. All we have to do to be able to live in his presence is be thankful. A broken heart and a contrite spirit only comes about through the stretching of the cross that causes the heart to be broken and then rupture. *God knows exactly how to put pressure on us to do something in us.*

Psalm 51:17 "The sacrifices of God are a broken spirit: a broken spirit and a contrite heart, O God, You will not despise." The opposite of despise is please. Only Jesus has the ability to please the Father. The Father said it twice in the Gospels. He said it for others to hear, not for Jesus to be secure. For he came from the bosom of the Father Jesus had no insecurities, he is our security. The Father said, *"This is my Beloved Son in whom I am well pleased"* If we are in him the Father is well pleased. For those who are not in Jesus await seven vials of wrath, not to mention everlasting unquenchable fire and utter darkness. The Hebrew word for broken used in Psalm 51 means burst or tear, and the Hebrew word contrite means to collapse. This was Jesus' actual bodily condition on the cross. Jesus is the only acceptable sacrifice the Father accepts. Abel offered the Blood of another, and God accepted it because it was true worship. Cain offered fruit from the cursed earth, and God rejected it. Pretty simple. The cross doesn't just stretch us to the max until our heartbreaks, but it does it publicly. We are hidden in Christ after the cross exposes and stretches us, and then breaks our heart and exposes the very framework of our being. Jesus was ripped open and beat and bleeding so badly, it is completely inconceivable. Though every Christian may not literally die on a cross physically, our flesh or self-life should be completely torn apart, as Jesus' body literally was before and on the cross.

Isaiah 52:17 "As many were astonished at You; His visage was so marred more than any man, and His form far more than the sons of men." The word astonished means to grow numb, to devastate, and destroy. Now we should see why John the Baptist said to "Behold the Lamb of God", well John the Revelator absolutely took his wise prophetic counsel. It is important not just to read the Bible but to study it, because it will study you also. The word "marred" in the previous scripture means disfigurement or corruption.

Jesus was so stretched and bleeding, theologians of old said he looked to be one big wound. His physical body was so bad the word corruption is also used, and he became the curse and took on our sin. He paid our price so the next time we want justice served on someone who mistreats us we should think of Jesus and remember mercy. The solution to every problem is simply seeing Jesus, for we will surely become what you behold. Everything changed when the disciples saw Jesus crucified. Now we have a generation who needs to be told to behold the Lamb of God. The most profound statement someone has ever said to me was, "Behold the Lamb of God." After that my whole life got turned upside down. Dr. Sandy Kirk is the woman that said that and it was the highest thing someone has ever said to me. The second highest thing someone has said to me was a swift rebuke, but that is another story for another day and right now we are beholding the Lamb of God, which is practice for heaven. Jesus is the center and we will marry a Lamb, not a King although he is a King, not a Military leader although he is the Lord of Hosts, but a Slain Lamb who bears wounds who alone is Worthy. While we are Beholding the Lamb, let us behold him with the Prophet, Priest and King David and see what he saw in *Psalm 22:17-18*. *"I may tell all my bones: they look and stare upon me. They part My garments among them, and they cast lots for my vesture."* David is gazing at a man whose bones are literally visible; he's been beat and stretched so bad his bones are visible. The suffering Jesus did to purchase us is incomprehensible! It needs to be talked about; it can no longer be hidden or unspoken of in the church. The cross is the drawbridge into the Kingdom. God is raising up a generation who will speak of who Jesus really is and how he really suffered. The Gospel must become personal once again if it is going to have its full affect on the church and eventually the world around us. The cross caused great pain and humiliation to all those who would be put to death on it. We must understand that no mercy was given to Jesus on the cross for when he was thirsty they gave him vinegar; he suffered at the hands of totally ruthless men. On top of the natural suffering, he was forsaken by his Father, who for all of Eternity past was never once separated from him. Jesus is on the cross bearing the Wrath of God and there is no mercy available to him, no one could help him. They are gambling for his clothes, so that is pretty clear that he has none on. This is a harsh and brutal thing to even think about. God himself was naked on a tree so we could be clothed with him. Jesus who's pure, holy and undefiled is hanging there as one big, naked wound ripped apart and bleeding. While he's hanging the people are gambling for his clothes, meanwhile he prays, "Father forgive them." This is unfathomable, incomprehensible and terrifying to even think about, he was stripped and beat and whipped so we could be clothed with light, so we can put on the Lord Jesus Christ, so we could be healed. For this we must be terribly grateful. When wrath comes it is the absence of mercy, he received no mercy, yet was still giving it to the other man on the cross and even those who were giving mocking him, gambling for his clothes and giving him vinegar. This further proves He was fully God and fully man! Jesus who was purity, holiness, blameless and undefiled was beaten, stripped, stretched and exposed. He literally became sin for us to be free from it. Friend, we shouldn't dabble in what caused Jesus to have to suffer like that. Let the kindness of his suffering for us completely change us from the inside out.

Chapter 3

The thorns, the nails, and the piercing

Many things happened to Jesus even before he went to the cross, the fact that he even made it to the cross alive most would say is a horrifying miracle. He was spat on in front of the High priest, who prophesied that Jesus would die for the sins of people that year. It is interesting how the High Priest Caiaphas prophesied about what Jesus would do, referring to Jesus dying for the nation, then shortly after spat on him. This is disrespect personified, this was so great a disrespect that the person who was spat on would have to go out side the camp to be cleansed (See Numbers 12:14) and so he did and to be crucified. Before he went out he suffered some horrible things and we will touch those things briefly, although it probably didn't feel so brief to Him.

Matthew 27:29-30 "And when they had platted a crown of thorns, they put it on his head, and a reed in His right hand: and they bowed the knee before Him, and mocked Him, saying, Hail, King of the Jews! And they spit upon Him, and took the reed, and smote Him on the Head." Jesus at this point has been beat by religion and a form of godliness that denies the power, and now he's being beat and spit upon by pagans. The Religious and the global empire is now beating him, he was so humble as to pay his taxes to Caesar, as to not offend those who would put him to death. There is no one like this man Jesus, he is love personified, and he is the living breathing truth. Now Jesus has a crown of thorns on Him and they hit him on the head, as to further drive the thorns into his head. Blood is dripping down his head and face. His head at this point is swollen to the max. He one day will be crowned with many crowns, but on this day his head is crowned with many thorns. During this time perhaps he's thinking of all the believers who will have his very mind. Perhaps Jesus is thinking of how worth it you are to him, and how bad he desires all people to know the thoughts he thinks toward them. The crown of thorns cost Jesus a lot but we receive the mind of Christ freely. That is the grace of God, Jesus paying for what we deserve and cannot earn. So he continues on because we were the joy set before him.

At this point Jesus can't even carry the cross, and now we see the grace of God in another unprecedented way. *Remember that it is the grace of God that makes his truth visible.* Jesus being fully God could have had the cross hover over his head and supernaturally been nailed to the cross, but rather his fully man side is suffering at this point.

Mind you he's fully God and fully man. His humanity and divinity is seen when the tempter satan comes to tempt Jesus in the wilderness. There Jesus says, *"man shall not live by bread alone, but by every word that proceeds from the mouth of God."* This statement is clearly revealing his humanity. Then he tells satan, *"Thou shall not tempt the Lord thy God."* This is revealing Jesus' deity to the devil himself. His divinity is also seen when Jesus was in Mary's womb and Elizabeth calls him *"Lord"*, see Luke 1:43. His divinity is also seen when he makes no apology for his parents getting ahead of God, when they left him in the temple. God will never apologize for who he is or what he does; however he will say, *"Blessed are those who are not offended in me."*

Mercy picks us up when we fall, grace helps us to stand. So the grace of God becomes visible and tangible when Simon of Cyrene, carries Jesus' cross for him. This to me is the best picture of grace ever in scripture, which is my humble opinion. Many believers have been taught false things about what grace is, so this is my favorite picture of grace in action. Soon Jesus is going to be pounded to a Tree, and this has all been of his free will. Jesus said, *"No man takes my life I lay it down."* Not only did he say that but he also illustrated manifesting his sovereignty and divine authority in the Garden of Gethsemane. *Psalms 1:5 KJV "Therefore the ungodly shall not stand in the judgment, nor sinners in the congregation of the righteous."* The ungodly or sinners cannot stand in the judgment. In the Gospel of John we learn that Jesus' death judges the world. *John 12:31-33 KJV "Now is the judgment of this world: now shall the prince of this world be cast out. And I, if I be lifted up from the earth, will draw all men unto me. This he said, signifying what death he should die."* Later in the book of John we see the Roman soldiers coming to get Jesus. *John 18:4-8 KJV "Jesus therefore, knowing all things that should come upon him, went forth, and said unto them, Whom seek ye? They answered him, Jesus of Nazareth. Jesus saith unto them, I am he. And Judas also, which betrayed him, stood with them. As soon then as he had said unto them, I am he, they went backward, and fell to the ground. Then asked he them again, Whom seek ye? And they said, Jesus of Nazareth. Jesus answered, I have told you that I am he: if therefore ye seek me, let these go their way:"* Jesus showed the Romans and all that were in the Garden that truly no man takes his life but he lays it down. They all fell down when they stepped into the atmosphere of the King uninvited. They fell because he was showing them and all generations that no man takes his life but he lays it down. In laying down his life he would have to die. His death would judge this world. So as the Savior was getting ready to give his life, sinners could not stand in the judgment.

The Holy Spirit whispered something to me one day and it was this, *"when you can no longer carry your cross, I will send someone to help you carry it for I am that passionate about killing you."* This blew me away; remember Jesus was forsaken by his Father. All of his followers dropped their crosses, which left only John the beloved and 4 women, his mom, her sister, Mary Magdalene, and Cleophas' wife, to show up at the cross. They were the five wise virgins who went out to meet the Bridegroom in the midnight hour, or the hour of adversity. As God sent someone to help Jesus carry his cross, Jesus' promise to us is, "I will never leave you nor forsake you", so when we can no longer carry our cross, Jesus will help us carry ours, even though our sin is what put him on his. The reason Jesus will help us carry our cross is so we can be worthy of him and so we can die to self, and live in him. Before we are alive to God we must be dead to sin. Jesus has pleasure forevermore, and a place prepared for us and its all worth it, just trust him enough to follow and obey. If we say Jesus is faithful or worthy and don't trust him, what exactly is he worthy of to us?

Matthew 27: 34 "They gave Him vinegar drink mingled with gall: and when he had tasted thereof he would not drink." This drink they tried to give him was like a numbing potion or like anesthesia to numb the pain, it was used to help relieve or alleviate one from pain, but he would not drink it. Jesus chose to lay down his life. Therefore no one took it or could have taken it, it had to be laid down. You can't kill God but He can choose to lay down his life for his friends, enemies, religious people, poor people, rich people, and all people who would bow their knee to him alone. Jesus is crowned with thorns and refuses to drink the painkiller, for he was shortly going to crush sickness, disease, pain, infirmity, and even death itself. So he is about to be crucified, let us look again and see it through King David's eyes roughly 1000 years before in *Psalm 22:16. "For dogs have compassed Me the assembly of the wicked have inclosed Me: they have pierced My hands and My feet."* The way David is describing this, it is as if he is in Christ looking down hanging on the cross giving a play by play from the eyes of Christ. David's vision becomes New Testament doctrine through Paul in Ephesians 1. *Ephesians 1:4 KJV "According as he hath chosen us in him before the foundation of the world, that we should be holy and without blame before him in love:"* David is not just having an open prophetic vision, he is seeing eternal truth from a divine perspective. This is accessible to us also through intimacy with Christ Jesus.

1 Peter 1:11 "Searching what manner of time the Spirit of Christ which was in them did signify, when it testified before hand the sufferings of Christ and the glory that should follow." The Holy Spirit is showing David from His perspective, since Holy Spirit lived in David, David saw it and spoke it in 3rd person not 1st person, quite interesting and a little controversial. I just believe what the Bible says, many want to study Greek, but don't even believe what is says in English. If we believe what it says in English and then study in Hebrew and Greek, we will get a whole lot deeper and further. So now we see through the eyes of David that Jesus is nailed to a Tree, the nails left permanent scars, forever scars, scars that Thomas was invited to stick his fingers in. *Isaiah 49:16 "Behold I have graven you upon the palms of My hands; your walls are continually before Me."* Thomas had the privilege of putting his hand where our very name is written, I am borderline jealous. The nails are no longer holding Jesus to the Tree but his hands bear the scar of his sacrifice forever. However the nails are still holding the accusations that were against us to the tree, according to Colossians 2:14, so we must be sure to leave them there.

During the time Jesus was nailed to the Tree, people were mocking him and trying to do anything to get him off that tree, but they couldn't. He would not save himself because he told us to deny ourselves, if he didn't he would have been a hypocrite and could not have died for us. Let us ponder together an attempt to get Jesus off the cross. *Luke 23:35 "And the people stood beholding. And the rulers also derided Him, saying, He saved others; let Him save Himself, if He be the Christ, the Chosen of God."* Right before this Jesus is praying to the Father, *"Father forgive them."* At this time no man has ever responded to a cross like this, I believe the forces of darkness at this time began to realize what they were doing and were trying to stop themselves from being deceived, but it was too late. *1 Corinthians 2:8 "Which none of the princes of this world knew: for had they known it they would not have crucified the Lord of Glory."* The deceiver doesn't just deceive others he is also deceived himself. We will either deny ourselves or deceive ourselves. Humility denies itself while pride deceives itself. Religion says save yourself, but Jesus gave himself as a ransom for the many. When Christ was nailed to the tree, there were mocking accusations of Him being King, as found in *Luke 23:36 "And the soldiers mocked Him, coming to Him, and offering Him vinegar, And saying, If you be the King of the Jews, save yourself."* What is interesting about their mocking accusations is that Jesus really was the King of the Jews.

The rulers of the religious world knew who Jesus was and they simply rejected him, the parable in Mark 12 concerning the vineyard makes it clear. For he was the stone the builders rejected. It was religion that crucified Jesus, and that same spirit comes to take the cross out of the church and replace Christ and him crucified with some other feel good gospel. While Jesus was on the cross he could have got off, but rather he chose to stay on. If death couldn't hold him, do you think nails can? He chose to commit himself to God's will of Him being given because God so loved the world.

While being nailed to the cross we have a choice to commit ourselves to God's sovereignty or behave like the thief who was still mocking and being arrogant. During the time of God's sovereignty, while we are nailed to a tree, is where the "works-based" mentality is broken off a Christian, because our hands are nailed to a cross therefore we can't do anything and our feet are nailed to a tree so we can't go anywhere. So before we live fruitfully we must die painfully. There are many Christians who are busy and worried about many things like Martha, the only way the accusations and the "works-based" mentality go is when we meet Jesus on the cross.

The enemy tempted Jesus in the wilderness, not to go to the cross; he offered Jesus everything yet Jesus refused. Jesus overcame the temptation of identity-based performance; therefore we must live in his victory which was for us. In the six hours of being nailed to the cross, slowly Jesus' was fully spilled out. While we are on the cross, we have a good amount of time to leave our old life behind and never return. I am trying to show the correlations of Jesus physicals sufferings to the Spiritual processes we go through in life. If we return to our old life we didn't let the cross do its job in killing us and we got off prematurely. Before we are taken off something draining must take place, when it does we have come through the working of the cross.

Let us look through the eyes of the disciple who Jesus loved. John the Beloved was the only man at the foot of the cross with four women. The Gospel of John is the only Gospel where it was recorded that a spear pierced Jesus' side. John beheld the Lamb of God at the foot of the cross, while he was taking away the sins of the world. I can imagine John weeping while remembering just days ago when he laid his head on Jesus' chest and heard the very heart beat that spoke the world into existence. Now his bones are visible and his blood is being shed slowly, and Jesus speaks to John and tells John to behold your Mother, speaking of Jesus' mom and entrusting John to take care of the woman who gave Birth to him. After the resurrection, Jesus calls his disciples brethren, but before His death John was a part of His family (see John 19:27, Matthew 28:10). This was the only specific person to be joined to Jesus' family while he was alive. Jesus did say that in his family are those who "do the will of my Father", but John was singled out because he was at the cross. He could be trusted to take care of the one who Jesus was subject to as a child. What a trust and honor that Jesus gave to John the Beloved, the place that John had in the heart of God is unthinkable. John remembers the sound of Jesus' heart beating, and now that same heart is broken and bleeding. The depth of John's thoughts at that time could have drowned a fish, through realizing the weight of the reality of the one who walked on water, the one who raised the dead, hanging there bleeding to death. At the same time being mocked and totally humiliated, naked in front of His mother. Bearing the Wrath of God, when all He did is give others mercy. What was John feeling? What was John thinking? Jesus said shortly after that, *"It is finished"* referring to the cup, and then gave up the Ghost. Remember Jesus wasn't killed he gave his life. Then the soldiers came to brake his legs and Jesus was already dead, even His death was a Miracle. After he was dead the soldiers pierced his side. John 19:34 *"But one of the soldiers with a spear pierced His side, and forwith came there out blood and water."* Even when Jesus' spirit was not in His body scripture was still being fulfilled, Scripture clearly shows that Jesus had offered His breath up. The soldiers didn't have to break His legs, nor could they because then prophecy would not have been fulfilled, but every jot and tittle will be fulfilled.

As we further look in to the piercing of Jesus we will also touch on a prophecy, which is also being fulfilled. Perhaps someone else is receiving their prophetic promise as Jesus is lifted up on a tree. We receive the piercing from the Sword of the Lord or the Word of God after we are dead. To truly be empty you must first die. Only dead men receive the piercing of the Word. When the Blood and the water poured out of Jesus' body it was like his blood was prophesying to the dust of the earth where all men came from saying, "you have been purchased". When the water touched the earth it was a token that He will pour out His Spirit on all flesh, as it says in Joel 2:28 "afterward".

During the time of Jesus' birth He was brought to the temple, and Simeon received His Prophetic promise that the Holy Ghost had revealed to him, concerning seeing the Lord's Christ. So Simeon is holding Jesus up and blessing Jesus, Joseph and Mary. While Jesus is being lifted up Simeon begins to prophesy to Mary. *Luke 2:34-35 "And Simeon blessed them, and said unto Mary His mother, Behold, this child is set for the fall and rising again of many in Israel and for a sign which shall be spoken against; Yes a sword shall pierce through your own soul also, that the thoughts of many hearts may be revealed."* Mary in the natural walked out the Christian life. She gave birth to the Messiah, Christ is to be formed in us and the expression and fruit comes from the womb, all fruitfulness come from intimacy, Children are made in Covenant, and the wedding bed is undefiled. Mary in the natural is a picture of all Christians who walk in the Spirit. God desires truth in the inward parts. While Jesus was lifted up Mary received her Prophetic promise of piercing, and I believe she received her prophetic promise when Jesus was lifted up on that Tree. The awesome part is this, when Jesus is lifted up some great stuff happens. As Jesus was lifted up and emptied out literally, I believe then Mary received the piercing, as promised to her by Simoen. The nature of why I believe this is because Jesus was being lifted up when she received the word, and Jesus prophesied to the man next to him and said *"today you will be with me in paradise."* That prophecy was while he was on the cross; you just can't stop Jesus from being who He is. He is ministering salvation while He is being condemned, who is like Him? Mary needed to be pierced just like any one else who wants to serve their master for life, we find this principle even in the Old Testament in the Book of Exodus the 21:1-6.

It is necessary that we experience the piercing and the pierced One. We cannot come off the cross until we are completely empty, and before we are emptied we must die. We cannot get ourselves off the cross or there would be no point of getting on it. The cross must mark us, stretch us, rupture our heart totally and expose all our flesh. The cross confronts the very framework of who we are, it must kill us and then we are ready to be emptied out and taken off. The cross is not only to be carried, but studied, and experienced. The piercing also has a Bridal revelation. Adam went to sleep and a woman was taken out of him from his very own rib. Jesus died on a cross, and was pierced and we come into Christ through His pierced side. Eve came out from Adam, and we come into Christ. Eve's actions and Adam becoming complacent and not taking His rightful role, cost Jesus His very life. Jesus spent Himself on a Bridal company, who will do Him good all the days of her life and the heart of her Husband safely trusts in her. Jesus suffered as a Bridegroom, which is even on one of His names. His value for us is so clearly seen. "Bride", who is us, and "Groom", which is Him. Us in Him, Christ in us, He ransomed His life for us. Therefore we must wholly give ourselves to him.

Chapter 4
The fellowship of his sufferings

Due to not really knowing or understanding what Jesus did, we for the most part have failed to become like Him. Much of the church has failed to preach the message of the Cross. The cross is hardly preached; it has even been taken out of large churches so as not to offend people. All this is wonderful for me to tell you, but telling you this is not at all the solution. The solution is for us to return to Jesus and the preaching of him and him crucified. The answer is very simple; preach the cross, preach Christ and Him Crucified, for it is the power of God unto salvation. Before we can preach the cross without being hypocrites we must know Jesus, meet Him on the cross, and be made conformable to His death. The cross is the best prevention for identity fraud. All Christians become Christians only through the Blood of Jesus, and only when we are crucified with Christ. If we don't die how can we ever be born again? I believe there is a realm of power that we as a church have not corporately tapped into because we haven't fully died to self. When we learn to die to self is when we learn how to love God and our neighbor. For a man to be born again He must die, the means of death is only a cross. It is the way Jesus died, or offered Himself up and in the Kingdom everything must be done the King's way. We are born again to see the Kingdom and to live from heaven towards earth. We are not born again if we are not crucified with Christ. The simplicity of Christ is the wineskin in which God can pour the mysteries of Christ in. The mysteries of the Kingdom are about the King, for everything in the Kingdom is a reflection of the King. His desire is for us to know Him and He wants to be fully formed in us, but first we must meet Him on the cross. The cross connects heaven and earth and God and man. Through the cross we can go to heaven because God came in the likeness of man in the person of Christ and gave himself for us.

Through Christ's sufferings we have fellowship. Christ did not only suffer and die for us, He modeled the very life we should live in and through Him who strengthens us. Every decision He ever made was for you and I, and to be an example to us of what we should and shouldn't do! For example, as soon as His disciple's would go to sleep, He would go up to the mountain and pray and spend time with the Father. A Christian's favorite thing should be to spend time with the Living God. We must learn to be branches that draw life directly from the True Vine himself. Before we are a useful member of a body we must become a branch that draws life directly from Jesus. Our favorite thing to do is what we consistently and diligently do on our free time. When Jesus had some free time, he didn't go in to the local bar and evangelize or to the local church and preach, He went up to the mountain and spent time with the Father. Unfortunately many Christians are not formed directly by their relationship with God. The majority of Christians are formed based on other people's opinions about God rather than their experiences with him. In Luke 10, Jesus had just finished rebuking Martha, then the next verse in Luke 11:1 His disciples ask Him to teach them how to pray. Dedication to spend time with God will provoke Him to reveal Himself to us. Dedication provokes revelation, just look at John at the cross and what He received on the Island of Patmos. John showed up in Jesus' darkest hour and Jesus entrusted him to see that he was the light of

God's heavenly city. *Revelation 21:23 KJV "And the city had no need of the sun, neither of the moon, to shine in it: for the glory of God did lighten it, and the Lamb is the light thereof."*

Jesus being perfect learned obedience through the things He suffered. If Jesus being perfect learned through suffering, and Jesus being the very embodiment of God's will, had to increase in Favor with God and man, how much more do we need to suffer and increase in Favor. These two are not separate, Scripture makes it clear that Daniel, and Jesus, had favor with God and men. Yet favor lead Jesus to a cross and Daniel to a Lion's den. The thing they both had in common is the stone was rolled away, for Daniel left without a scratch and Jesus left with wounds and holes, but nevertheless they both had favor. When we are identified with Christ we experience suffering. When the Word becomes flesh in us we experience persecution. *"All who live Godly in Christ Jesus shall suffer persecution"*, that's what Paul said to his spiritual son Timothy to prepare Him for what was to come. When we are persecuted for righteousness sake we are identified with Jesus. This is a glorious privilege, where fellowship abides in a Mystery and the knowledge of God is released. Favor and suffering are interesting combination. Joseph had so much favor with God and his Father that his brothers sold him into slavery. True favor on someone's life may just cause others to be jealous. Jealousy often gives birth to betrayal. Remember if you want to be crucified you first must be betrayed. *Matthew 26:2 KJV "Ye know that after two days is the feast of the Passover, and the Son of man is betrayed to be crucified."* When we pray, "Lord, we want to be just like you", we are asking to be betrayed. If we are going to live faithfully before God we will be betrayed.

Christ's sufferings paid for some very costly gifts. What has been given freely to us cost Jesus everything. Jesus is a big spender, He spent Himself on us and in doing that He purchased us the very best. He has unsearchable riches and we have access to all that is his by the veil of his flesh through faith. Jesus bought us His very mind. The mind of Christ was purchased for us and the cost was a crown of thorns. Those thorns were pounded into His head. Most Christians disregard what goes on their head, not discerning it is the mind of Christ at work in them. We have been given the mind of Christ so we can hear God when he is silent and also see from his perspective. When our soul and spirit hasn't been divided often we lack discernment in recognizing God's voice. There is an order in the way God executes His will, even in someone dying; it all must be God's way. Jesus even prophesied the order of His sufferings in Mark 10: 33- 34

"Behold, we go up to Jerusalem and the Son of Man shall be delivered unto the chief Priests, and unto the scribes; and they shall condemn Him to death, and shall deliver Him to the Gentiles: And they shall mock Him, and spit upon Him, and shall kill Him: and the third day he shall rise again." There is an order to suffering, and even an order to the cross. God's will is accomplished His way, in His order, and in His timing. The cost of Jesus being able to know what temptation feels like cost Him meeting the Devil face to face. *Fasting breaks the bands of wickedness. Jesus fasts for forty days, he had no wickedness so the devil appears when he fasted.* Jesus had no wickedness, so the root and source of wickedness himself appears, only to have to flee. Isaiah 53:3 *"He is despised and rejected of men; a man of sorrows, and acquainted with grief: and we hid our faces from Him; He was despised, and we esteemed him not."* He was despised and rejected, so that we can be loved and accepted. There is such a cost to what Jesus freely gives us, *understanding the price Jesus paid is the only way to understand our true value to Him.* Understanding what He did brings us into the light of who he is and the Revelation on who we are in

him. When we come to truly know Jesus is when we learn to love him and one another. When we know him and love him we suddenly learn how to treat each other. When people don't know how to relate to others and are not sure how to receive people, it just simply shows that they don't truly know Jesus. We should only esteem one another more highly then ourselves, because Jesus did when He gave Himself for us. The Cross of Jesus is seen very clearly in our relationships as Christians, when we prefer one another and serve one another. A Christian who is not a radical giver in time, finances and resources, probably never had a real encounter with a Crucified Jesus. Many have been offended by people talking about money from the pulpit, or perhaps people being hoodwinked by some slick preacher, who won't be so slick when he stands before the Great White throne. If you have let some of this bad teaching or misrepresenting of Jesus from the pulpit affect your giving, you have been offended and your heart is slowly getting cold. Therefore you need to repent, just as much as the preacher who took your money and used it for something else, both are guilty. The cross crucifies our right to be offended. Offense happens when instead of feeling compassion for someone because of his or her foolish behavior we think we have the right to be angry or offended when we are mistreated. Our only right is the privilege to forgive others who don't deserve it and perhaps haven't even asked for it. True forgiveness doesn't wait for someone to ask to be forgiven; it just gives it away because the giver has so freely received it from Jesus. Jesus Cried out from the cross "father forgive them, for they know not what they do." What is interesting is none of them had asked to be forgiven. After Jesus' death the roman soldier at the foot of the cross knew he was the Son of God. The reason is that when he released forgiveness it empowered repentance, which led to the roman soldier knowing by revelation that Jesus was the Son of God. *Remember forgiveness works repentance and repentance opens the door of revelation.* All lasting change begins first by revelation.

The cry of dereliction from the cross was the cost for us to receive the Spirit of Adoption. The cry of dereliction is when Jesus screamed *"my God, My God why have your forsaken me."* Jesus was forsaken by His Father so we would never be. The pain of separation from His Father probably outweighed His physical pain. The pain that Jesus went through is probably the most inconceivable thing possible to be spoken about to the human mind.

I Corinthians 2:10 KJV "But God hath revealed them unto us by his Spirit: for the Spirit searcheth all things, yea, the deep things of God." Only the Holy Spirit can give us a glimpse of something that deep.

Romans 13:14 KJV "But put ye on the Lord Jesus Christ, and make not provision for the flesh, to fulfill the lusts thereof." The privilege to be able to put on the Lord Jesus cost him to be stripped and exposed on a Tree. Remember everyone in the Kingdom wears Jesus. The ability for us to be vulnerable with one another was paid for as Jesus hung fully exposed. Even His bones to be visible for the world to see, you are pretty vulnerable when you cannot go anywhere and you're pounded to a Tree that's on a hill for the world to see. The veil of His flesh was torn so we could have access to the Holy of Holies. The Holy of Holies had no entrance point. There was no slit in the veil. *John 6:44 KJV "No man can come to me, except the Father which hath sent me draw him: and I will raise him up at the last day."* Coming to Jesus and entering into the Holy of Holies has one thing in common. If the Father does not draw one, one cannot come. Every time a High Priest was translated through the veil supernaturally, it was based on the eternal merit of Jesus the Lamb who was slain from before the foundation of the world. It is through the veil of his flesh that we enter the presence of God. In the Holy of Holies is the place where God would speak to the high priest. The flesh of Jesus was also torn so that our ears would hear the voice of God. We have full access to God's presence and his voice. His presence comes to take residence from us and he speaks with us. The nearness of God came because of the eternal separation that happened with Jesus and the Father after the cry of dereliction. We must live forever grateful for what Jesus has done for us. Our lifestyle should communicate gratitude.

John 14:27 KJV "Peace I leave with you, My peace I give unto you: not as world giveth, give I unto you. Let not your heart be troubled, neither let it be afraid." This to me is so profound you can't have the peace of God and be afraid or troubled. The word troubled in that verse means agitate, if we are agitated we are being disobedient. Peace guards the Word of God in our hearts and minds. The cost of Peace was very high, *Isaiah 53:5 "But He was wounded for our transgressions, He was bruised for our iniquities: and the chastisement of our peace was upon Him; and with His stripes we are healed."* Jesus deeply suffered rebuke and chastisement for us to have peace. Often times, we freely give it away when someone says something we don't like or does something that's wrong. Jesus was tortured; his beard was ripped out of his face for our peace. Giving away what Jesus paid such a dear price for is just plain sinful. Do we really value Jesus? Or have we, as a people, been ignorant of the cost He paid? Everything Jesus gives us in the Kingdom was paid for on the cross. Our understanding of the Kingdom will be determined by our revelation of the cross. Have we yet to understand that Jesus is the biggest spender ever. Remember it was Jesus who was the merchant man who sold everything to buy the pearl in the field. The more we know what Jesus has done for us the more we will love him and hate sin. Jesus was wounded because of sin and will forever bear the marks of our sin. For our names to be graven upon his hand, our sin had to be put upon him. In timeless eternity we will have to look upon his scared body, which is his proof of our purchase. I believe Glory leaks from those wounds.

If the Lamb is the Light of the city and the Lamb is wounded as a Lamb having been slain, then eternal Light leaks from the wounds of our Bridegroom. When we marry the Lamb, there will be no need for artificial lighting because eternal Light will permeate from His very being. Jesus told his disciples if the house is worthy, let your peace rest on it. We have became His house and He's paid for His peace to rest upon us, and not because we are worthy but because he is worthy. Those who are worthy of Him carry their cross, even the disciples dropped their cross and didn't meet Jesus at His, so how about us? We are absolutely unworthy, which is why He does it because He's worthy. It was His choice to purchase us and wash us in His very own Blood.

Let's talk about Healing briefly. Physical healing illustrates something even greater and that is forgiveness. Forgiveness is what The Blood of Jesus speaks. The blood preaches the greatest sermon ever. The Blood of Cain cries out for Justice and the Blood of Jesus screams, *"You will not love your life because I gave mine for you."* I believe no voice to be louder than the Blood of Jesus. The Blood of Jesus has a voice and it says, "Behold the Lamb of God who takes away the sins of the world". So the temporary healing of our bodies is made available through the stripes on Jesus' back. Jesus has eternal stripes for our temporary healing. That is how much he loves us. Sickness to our body is like sin to our soul. In the Kingdom of God there is no sin and no sickness, therefore what Jesus has done for us on Calvary is made available to us now by faith. Not to have Faith is a sin of the deepest kind, because Jesus died in Faith that men and women would accept His sacrifice. He already knew who would and who wouldn't accept his sacrifice. He is the Author and the Finisher of the Lambs book of Life. If someone says I don't believe in healing for today, I would ask that person is God a Liar? Is Jesus Christ not the same yesterday today and forever? Do you value your lack of experience more than what the Scriptures teach? And are those wounds on Jesus not enough for you? Sometimes asking questions is wiser than just making statements. Look at the Lamb in the center of the Throne as having been slain, look at those wounds and see His value system and know you are His value system. All the people in the world that feel worthless feel this way because they've never experienced the Crucified Jesus. The price of Redemption that Jesus has paid can even redeem time because He was the Lamb Slain from before the foundation of the World before time was. Jesus death literally splits time itself in half. That is why time is measured in B.C, or before Christ, and A.D, after death or after the death of Christ. Delegated authority measured time in the Bible, specifically the King who was ruling at the time. Here are a few examples Isaiah 1:1, Isaiah 6:1, Jeremiah 1:3 etc. All authority has been given to Jesus therefore all time must be measured by him.

Hebrews 12:2 "Looking unto Jesus the Author and Finisher of our Faith; who for the Joy that was set before Him endured the cross, despising the shame, and is set at the right hand of God." The Joy of the Lord is what causes us to endure the cross. Joy is one of greatest expressions of life. To those who inherit eternal life Jesus says to them *"come and enter into the joy of your master."* Jesus was condemned so we would not have to be. We don't have to be if we walk not after the Flesh because Jesus gave his and it was sinless and completely sanctified. We were the Joy that was set before Him. The wages of Sin are death, for sin demands a payment and it is death. Jesus said sure thing, "I will empty myself out so they can be filled up. Yes I will be ripped apart so they can be whole. Absolutely, I will model for them how to put no confidence in the flesh, and totally be led by my Father. Yes, I will humble myself and be put to death by my creation, on my creation, for my creation. Yes absolutely, I will fast for 40 days and show them how to deny their flesh. Sure I will teach them fervent prayer, to the point of sweating Blood in the Garden." A man who needed a Savior baptized Jesus who was eternally perfect. The Jordan River was where John the Baptizer preached repentance. Jesus being perfect had no need of Repentance yet he was identifying with our condition because our sin was going to be put upon him. *Matthew 3:15 KJV "And Jesus answering said unto him, Suffer it to be so now: for thus it becometh us to fulfill all righteousness. Then he suffered him."* John was a Levite who never ministered in Jerusalem or in the temple. However for the law to be fulfilled a Levite had to consecrate the Lamb for Passover and so he did accomplishing all righteousness. God worked outside the religious box of the temple, but within the wisdom of his word.

Knowing about Christ's sufferings is not enough we should live in the Reward of His suffering, which is the outpouring of Holy Spirit. As we live in the reward of his Suffering we can bring him the reward of His suffering. The reward of His suffering is that the Holy Spirit would be poured out on us, so that we would bring people into the kingdom so the Father's would be full and Jesus would receive the nations as his inheritance. As we move forward in the purposes of God we will be tested and even persecuted, and at other times will be blessed and celebrated. What Jesus did on the cross was enough for the whole world to come into the Kingdom. The harvest is truly plentiful but the laborers are few. I believe you will be a faithful laborer in the Lord's harvest field. The fellowship of Christ's suffering is not only physical suffering or persecution. We sense the fellowship of Christ's suffering when we live with an unfulfilled God given longing. Keep in mind that Jesus only did what he saw the Father do and only said what he heard the Father say. *Matthew 23:37 KJV "O Jerusalem, Jerusalem, thou that killest the prophets, and stonest them which are sent unto thee, how often would I have gathered thy children together, even as a hen gathereth her chickens under her wings, and ye would not!"* Jesus desired to gather Jerusalem because the Father desired to gather Jerusalem, but Jerusalem didn't gather. This unfulfilled God given longing is another type of suffering. This kind of suffering often is very painful. In the times of living with unfulfilled God given longings we must guard our heart. Jesus' heart was ruptured and poured out so we can have a new heart. Therefore we must guard our heart from this kind disappointment and give it to the Lord in intercession. Disappointment can really infect a heart so we must have the breastplate of righteousness on at all times, which protects our new heart of flesh that Jesus paid so much for us to have. Jesus tasted death for every man so we could taste and see that he is good. He is not willing that any should perish according to 2 Peter 3:9. However people are perishing everyday. He desires them and paid for humanity, and it is our job to reach them. The key to a sustainable lifestyle of evangelism is a revelation of the cross. I am praying that God would pierce your heart with the sacrifice of Jesus Christ forever

Chapter 5
The measurements of love

What Jesus has done for us is so profound and deep that it will take ages to begin to get into the depth of it all. There are two main and simple character traits of the Father and the Son, with the operation of the Mighty Holy Spirit, which made the Cross of Jesus possible. Behind all Jesus' external suffering there was something in the Father that caused Him to send His Son, and something in the Son that said yes to the Father from before the foundation of the world. These are very important to understand because these are what the Spirit world sees. Remember a tree is known by its fruit. The Spirit world sees who we really are and who we are really not. The importance of carrying the cross is profound. When a NHL Hockey team wins the Stanley cup finals the winning team gets to hold the Stanley cup. That is a sign of victory. When we carry our crosses that is a sign of Christ's victory over death and the powers that be, and the law that condemned us. The cross is the most painful part of God's wisdom. *Colossians 2:14-15 "Blotting out the handwriting of ordinances that was against us, which was contrary to us, and took it out of the way, nailing it to his cross; And having spoiled principalities and powers, he made a show of them openly, triumphing over them in it."* What the enemy thought to be his biggest victory was his greatest defeat, now we see why he is called the deceiver. Remember a deceiver tends to be an accuser so we must be careful and make sure we become an advocate for others before God, as Jesus has done for us in his great kindness. The Spirit world knows who we are. An evil spirit said to the seven sons of sceva in *Acts 19:14 "And the evil spirit said, Jesus I know, and Paul I know; but who are you."* Those who are not crucified with Christ are not recognized in the Spirit.

John 3:16 "For God so loved the world that he gave his only begotten Son, that whosoever believes in him should not perish but have everlasting life." It is the Love the Father had that caused him to give his Son, if you are not a giver you are not a lover. All lovers are radical givers all around the board; it is like their whole life is a two-hour long offering that offends every greedy religious spirited person around them. Giving is one of the most offensive things one can do. God gave Jesus and the offense of the cross is so great it causes persecution to arise. So love gives and humility obeys.

The character that made the outward suffering of the cross possible was Love and Humility. It was the Father's Love and the Son's Humility. Love and humility are the characters of the cross. Love and humility are what facilitate true and sustainable unity. *Philippians 2:8 "And being found in fashion as a man, he humbled himself, and became obedient unto death, even the death of a cross."* Humility is what caused Jesus to participate with love and made the cross possible. If we are going to carry the cross and die on it, we must be full of love and humility. Love commissions and humility executes. Love gives and humility goes. The power of love and humility working in unity is larger and more powerful than anything on this earth. *Jonathan Edwards said this about humility, "Nothing sets a person so much out of the devils reach as humility."* These two attributes can never be separated if God's will is going to be executed God's way. In God's will, his ways are found and yet they are unsearchable which is why there is the Mystery of His will according to Ephesians 1:9.

Unsearchable ways, The Mystery of His will, Joy unspeakable, His unsearchable Riches, Jesus is the most Glorious and Fascinating person I have ever known. I can spend all day pondering quietly the brilliance of the Light that radiates off His face that gives light to the world, who is Like Him?

Love and Humility made the cross happen, and joy allows it to be endured. This is good news. Love casts out all fear, and humility is the antithesis of pride, God resists the proud but gives grace to the humble. When we are truly humble there is no resistance or distance between God and us. Humility makes us completely irresistible to God. We then become like the Jesus who lives in us. Love has measurements, when God does things he gives precise measurements. When the temple was to be built in Solomon's day, there were exact measurements. When Noah's ark was built there was again exact measurements. New Jerusalem, the city of God, has exact measurements. The measurements are precise. Only a little wood separated Noah from those who would receive the judgment of God. As it is even today, just some wood and some nails from more than two thousand years ago separate those who will be condemned to death, from those who will have life everlasting. Love has measurements; we will look at them together.

Ephesians 3:17-19 KJV "That Christ may dwell in your hearts by faith; that ye, being rooted and grounded in love, May be able to comprehend with all the saints what is the breadth, and the length, and depth, and height; And to know the Love of Christ, which passeth knowledge, that ye might be filled with all the fullness of God."

Many are rooted in love, but very few are grounded in love. When one is rooted the roots look strong on the surface but when the winds of adversity blow many bow to their adversary the devil, because their tree is not grounded. If you have ever seen a tree with big thick roots on the earth's surface, just check a tree like that after a hurricane and it will probably be upside down. Those who are rooted endure the storms and are there for others; their roots go down perhaps as deep as their tree is high. We must be rooted and grounded. Our roots and fruits are inseparable. Paul wants us to comprehend with all the saints, but why? What would be accomplished through this comprehension? We must ask ourselves this. I believe this comprehension will bring us into unity of the Spirit, and to the place where we deeply understand what Christ Jesus did on the tree. Then we will become willing to suffer if need be for him and one another. If we would know the love of Christ, we must receive a revelation of the cross for the cross is the greatest expression of love. If we were to measure a Cross it would have three measurements, Height meaning up and down, Width, meaning left to right, and the thickness or depth. To be able to comprehend it, we must be willing to get on it. We must come through the veil of His Flesh to enter the Holy of Holies, where the light of God's face shines when he speaks.

There is an order to approach God, for we approach Him on His terms because He is the Lord. Paul wants all the saints to come upon the Love of Christ, which surpass science or knowledge. Knowledge puffs up but revelation causes us to lie down and bow at the feet of Jesus. Paul wants all the saints to come upon the very place where Christ spent Himself on us so we can know him at the place of purchase. This is a man, Paul, who bears the scars of service. Paul bore the marks of the cross on his body, this is not a theory or a good idea, and Paul paid a price to write this. He was the offering, and these words are to be taken with the utmost respect. *God's word is to be trembled at, not tripped over.* Jesus is the stone of stumbling and the rock of offense, it is a terrifying thing for people to trip over the one who laid down his life. If Jesus is a rock of offense to us, or to those around us, it is simply because we have not comprehended or came upon the cross ourselves. The cross where his love is displayed. Dead men are not offended. We must die and be resurrected with Christ, and apprehended to his heavenly calling. *We are apprehended to comprehend*, Paul speaks about being apprehended.

That is what is needed in this hour, an apprehended crucified company who will preach the cross, carry the cross, and walk worthy of the Lord because the worthy one lives in us. The ramifications of a man, who was fully God and fully man and who thought it not to be robbery to be equal with God, hanging, dying and rising again has such everlasting effects on the human soul. Six hours of torture beyond human understanding stuns me and tenderizes my heart as I ponder the greatness of the Lord Jesus. The measurements of his love are so deep, high, wide and profound. Nothing can separate us from the love of God that is towards us through Christ Jesus. Jesus who was a carpenter while he was on the earth had to be an expert in the realm of measurement, and it is His desire for us to understand the measurements of his love. His love was shed for us on the cross. That same love is shed abroad in our hearts by faith as we deny ourselves, take up our cross, and follow Him. The long dusty road of sacrifice is a road that leads to great glory in the kingdom of God after we have passed through the straight gate. Remember it is the narrow way that leads to the straight gate because it is through much tribulation that we enter into the kingdom of God. The suffering of the cross for Jesus was six hours; the cross for us is daily. He was forsaken on His cross, but on ours we meet him and learn the measurements of His Love through the fellowship of his suffering. God works death in us as we wait on him. Jesus hung there naked for six hours waiting for scripture to be fulfilled. He was there for a very strategic six hours because he was the morning and the evening offering.

Carpenters use measurements all day long; a measurement that is just a quarter of an inch too long is useless. For about twelve hours a day for roughly eighteen years Jesus took measurements. The value of his carpentry was determined by the accuracy of his measurements. Value is what something is worth, but the cost is what one will have to pay to get it. Jesus counted the cost for eighteen years, as he made a living with wood, knowing one day he would give His life on a wooden cross. He knew one day, he wouldn't be nailing the wood, but would be nailed to it. Every day that Jesus worked this reality gripped Him, and everyday He said Yes Father, Your will not mine. I could just see Him as a young man so focused; on His purpose others probably could never understand Him. He's altogether not like us, for He was Blameless, and Spotless, the Son of God, and the Son of Man. I would like you to ponder this measurement. *Psalm 103:12 KJV "As far as the east is from the west, so far hath he removed our transgressions from us."* This speaks about that He; Jesus separated our transgressions as far as the east is from the west. What's so profound is that is a measurement but its impossible to comprehend unless you know the center or the point where you would begin the measurement from. Jesus is the center, and His love is the measurement. Ponder the distance of your sin, which the blood of Jesus has forever washed away. Christ became the propitiation and paid our debt in full. Think of how far our sin is from us, to try to return to it would be so foolish. It's so far and besides sin really expensive and a lot of hard work, and the wages aren't that good. We are completely debt free to sin because of what Jesus has done. However we owe the world an encounter with God and we owe God the world he died for.

Chapter 6
When darkness covered all the earth

Jesus said I am the Light of the World, which is true. I really believe what Jesus has said. However, I don't just believe what Jesus has said, I believe what He is saying because we live by the word that is proceeding from his mouth. *John 1:4 KJV "In him was life; and the life was the light of men."* The light that Jesus is, also contains life. Paul spoke about Jesus dwelling in unapproachable light, yet while he was on the cross darkness covered the face of the whole earth. Jesus dwells in light unapproachable, yet that light was put out when the wrath of God consumed on the tree. The light of the world became the burnt offering. The meaning of the burnt offering is "the Holocaust offering." That's what burnt means in Hebrew, Jesus is familiar with every kind of suffering known to man. Father God knows what it feels like to out-live His Precious Son. There is not a tragedy that Jesus hasn't felt or cannot be with you through, if you call upon Him with a sincere heart.

I want you to imagine an unapproachable light on the cross, just there surrounding Jesus from every angle, then an all consuming Fire from heaven totally consuming that un approachable light until that light is no more. Picture Jesus the vine, on the tree and the wrath of God consuming that vine until it was burned to ashes. Jesus in a cup drank our hell, so we don't have to go there. He became the curse so we don't have to live under it. He paid sin's wages in full so you can invest in another Kingdom.

When Jesus said I am the Light of the World, he proved it when He said let there be light and there was light, see Genesis 1:3. Later the natural light was created and it separated day from night, see Genesis 1:14-16. Jesus doesn't just say stuff. He often does something and then puts language to what He has already done. The unapproachable light, who is life, gave his life and drank utter darkness in a cup for us. He drank the Cup of the Wrath of God. He paid everyone's sin loan; all we have to do is come to him.

Jesus proves that He was the Light of the World, and it is so interesting how many things that were happening, and had already happened while Jesus is hanging on a tree. He appeared to be helpless, to the carnal eye. Who else can save people while they're being condemned, only someone who is fully God and fully man, Jesus Christ of Nazareth, Son of God, Son of Man. Those who do not except Jesus, who bought them, will be cast in to utter darkness. Utter darkness came upon Jesus while He drank the Cup, which He absolutely did not deserve but willingly drank so that we could taste and see that he is good. In John 9, Jesus makes a profound statement, which fascinates my Heart. *John 9:5 "As long as I am in the world, I am the Light of the world."* At this moment Jesus is about to spit in clay, rub spit and clay into a blind man's eyes and give Him his sight for the first time. Jesus was really pushing the envelope on religion on that one. Remember religion is what Crucified Jesus, so if you are crucified with Him, religion must go and it is replaced with the ways of God. Spit, under the Law, made someone unclean and they would have to go outside the camp for a time. However Jesus was clean and he went outside the camp to make us clean. The Pharisees accused Jesus of breaking the Law, yet he gave it and fulfilled it. The religious leaders couldn't see that. The Pharisee's, Sadducees, and Scribes all read the same exact book of the Law yet lived different and believed different, but they all could agree on putting Jesus to death. Religion is a real ugly spirit. Religion can go to the right Church, read the right Bible, and pray the right prayer. Yet Religion could never know who Jesus really is or perceive what he is doing. Religion waits to accuse and tries to use Jesus' words to do so, see Luke 11:54. Religion does not want you to know the crucified Jesus; religion hates the preaching of the cross, because it condemned Jesus unto its own defeat.

So Jesus is hanging on the Tree, bleeding, bones exposed, in total humiliation, and He's drinking the cup. Jesus didn't need hands to drink of this cup. So he's there on the Tree and something very profound is happening. *Luke 23:44-46 "And it was about the sixth hour and there was darkness over all the earth until the ninth hour. And the sun was darkened, and the veil of the temple was rent in the midst."* I believe those three hours were when Jesus drank the cup, and the cup had to be finished before Jesus could offer up His Spirit. When Jesus offered up His Spirit the whole earth was dark. Remember what He said, "as long as I am in the world, I am the light of it", and so as he goes so does the light. Jesus drank utter darkness; He became sin for us so that we didn't have to be a slave to it. While Jesus is doing this in the Spiritual realm or the unseen, the seen world is reflecting what is happening in the unseen, because the unseen is greater. One of the men, who probably helped crucify Jesus, is glorifying God. History states that His name was Longinus and he became a follower of Christ and also a Martyr. That is the way God works: help kill Jesus and then die for Him. Like Paul persecuting Jesus and then being persecuted for Him, putting Stephen to death and then later willingly giving His life for Jesus. Jesus is leaving the world and so is the light, all this happens to prove to everyone who He is; I bet that blind man remembered what Jesus had said about him being the light of the world and then seeing all the light leave the world as he was being crucified. I would love to know what that man who had received His sight was thinking when the whole world looked like his previous life experience of being blind, for those three hours

In scripture we are told to walk in the Light as He is in the Light, if we understand the price Jesus paid we can be where He is, we would then learn to walk worthy of the Lord. Before we could walk in the Light, the Light had to become sin, pay the penalty, and conquer death and the grave so we can be free from it. As believers, we need to beholders who behold the Lamb of God. Before we can walk in the light he laid down His life and became our darkness, so we would not have to be cast there. Light is a person and if we are in Him, His Light is in us making us His reflection. When Jesus looks at you He sees the Spirit that raised Jesus from the dead, if you are a believer in Him. This light shines in the darkness and the darkness does not overcome it.

The Father reveals Christ in his timing and in perfect order. In John, Jesus is revealed as the light of the world. In the book of Revelation, Jesus is the light of the city of God. Revelation is progressive because we are on a journey of all truth. The journey beings at the cross, and leads to the Kingdom. We have to be crucified with Christ before we can be born again. For someone to be born again someone has to die. We are born again to see the Kingdom. The cross is the drawbridge into the Kingdom. When Jesus gave himself for us, all that he is and has became ours because we are now in him. In the Kingdom of God there is an international anthem and it is, "Worthy is the Lamb that was slain." The anthem song of the Kingdom is about what the King did to get us into his glorious kingdom. We are citizens from above, but we must never forget what Jesus did for us on the earth that we might be his royal citizens.

Chapter 7
Jesus speaks from the cross

The Holy Spirit whispered something to me one day; it was something like this, *"You can learn the most about someone in their darkest, weakest and most vulnerable hour, just look at Jesus on the Cross."* This totally messed me up. The Holy Spirit is so passionate about Jesus. The mighty Holy Spirit's favorite topic is Jesus. If Jesus were to write books, the Holy Spirit would write a commentary of every book Jesus writes. Mr. Holy Spirit longs to reveal Jesus, I can't even imagine or begin to describe His passion for Jesus. Without Holy Spirit we have no passion for Jesus. Holy Spirit convicts us and brings us to the cross where Jesus offered him up to the Father. Holy Spirit will always take us to the place where Jesus offered Him up, so we can lay down our life and experience who Jesus really is.

In Revelation 4:5 and Revelation 5:6 there is something established that is important for us to understand. *Revelation 4:5 KJV "And out of the throne proceeded lightnings and thunderings and voices: and there were seven lamps of fire burning before the throne, which are the seven Spirits of God."* Here we see the Seven Spirits of God burning before the throne of God. *Revelation 5:6 KJV "And I beheld, and, lo, in the midst of the throne and of the four beasts, and in the midst of the elders, stood a Lamb as it had been slain, having seven horns and seven eyes, which are the seven Spirits of God sent forth into all the earth."* Here we see the Lamb with the seven eyes, and seven horns. The seven eyes are for sight and the seven horns are for sound. You can see and hear the Seven Spirit's manifesting even in the Gospels. Jesus had the Spirit with out measure, He had the Seven fold manifestation or expression of the Holy Spirit, and it is awesome to see them manifesting through his life and ministry. When Jesus speaks from the Cross we can see some of this pretty clearly if Holy Spirit so chooses to illuminate and fascinate our hearts with the Lamb and His Seven Spirits.

Jesus is now hanging naked from a tree stretched to the max, ripped apart, and his bones are visible but not broken. He is being totally humiliated. No one any where on either side of eternity can help Him, for this purpose has he come. When Jesus was being condemned and mocked, He had a burden to Pray. His prayer was *"Farther forgive them"* in Luke 23:34, this is the manifestation of the *Spirit of Intercession*, or that of Grace and Supplication according to Zechariah 12:10. Jesus is interceding for someone while he is hanging in the gap for all of humanity. Jesus is the only mediator between God and man, and he ever lives to make intercession for us even while he was dying.

Then a Few verses later, the Father answered His prayer. In Luke 23:43, Jesus' prayer gets answered. His Father gives Him the ok; remember Jesus only does what He sees the Father do. Then Jesus says to the thief *"Today you shall be with me in paradise."* This was a direct answer to Jesus' prayer. It is interesting how a thief saw a naked man bleeding to death on a tree and called him "Lord" and asked Jesus to "remember him in his kingdom." The cross is the drawbridge into the Kingdom. When the cross is revealed the Kingdom of heaven becomes accessible. The revelation of the cross gives us understanding to operate in the Kingdom and reveals the value of our inheritance that is in Christ Jesus. Also there are two other of the seven-fold expressions at work here. The Spirit of Prophecy is the Testimony of Jesus and what this does, is it opens up Heaven. This is clearly seen in *Revelation 19: 10b-11a "The Testimony of Jesus is the Spirit of Prophecy. And I saw Heaven opened."* Heaven Opens and John sees Jesus. The Spirit of Prophecy opens Heaven and puts Jesus on display. The Spirit of Prophecy reveals the Supremacy of Christ. Yet without Holiness no man can see the Lord, let alone be where He is.

It is the *Spirit of Holiness*, which gives this man on the cross next to Jesus access to heaven. The Spirit of Holiness is seen in *Romans 1:4 KJV "And declared to be the Son of God with power, according to the spirit of holiness, by the resurrection from the dead:"* It is the Spirit of Holiness that raised Jesus from the dead. This man was dead in His trespasses but through the blood of Jesus he was given the resurrection of the dead and now became alive to God. He was in Paradise that day as Jesus had prophesied from the cross. Here the Sprit of Prophecy opened up heaven and the Spirit of Holiness made him alive to God.

Jesus at this point is still on the cross, bleeding for us and He says a few more things that I will share for edification. The truest and purest form of edification is the revelation of Jesus Christ. Telling someone what is wrong with him or her may not change him or her, but when one's Spirit man sees Jesus for who he really is, then change is right around the corner. Let us behold the Lamb of God, who at this point is becoming the sins of the world so as to purge us with His precious Blood from all of our sin and iniquity. When Jesus says to John the revelator in John 19:27 behold your mother, and to Mary behold your son. This is the Working of the *Spirit of Adoption*. Jesus refers to John the revelator as brother. He does not specifically call His disciples Brethren until after He rose from the dead, but if you show up to the cross you get some special privileges. God is not a respecter of persons, but there was only one Joseph in Egypt and one Daniel in Babylon. If you press in you will get more from God. *The Spirit of Adoption* was given to us. The cost was the Cry of Dereliction from Jesus. The cry of dereliction is what theologian's call when Jesus cried out, *"my God my God why have you forsaken me."* There is a progression in our relationship with Jesus if we deny ourselves daily and take up cross and follow Him. We go from disciples and then He calls us friends, making all things known to us. Then we become His brother, as we do the will of His Father. The Father's business is to reveal his Son in and through us.

The *Spirit of Burning and Judgment* was consuming Jesus while he was on the tree. *Isaiah 4:4 KJV "When the Lord shall have washed away the filth of the daughters of Zion, and shall have purged the blood of Jerusalem from the midst thereof by the spirit of judgment, and by the spirit of burning."* The Spirit of burning and judgment was Jesus' blood dropping onto the soil washing away the filth of the daughters of Zion. This made Jerusalem the most valuable place in the world because the blood of God himself touched the very soil in which his name is written. He was being consumed for our sins. When Jesus had finished the Cup of Wrath He made a simple and very profound statement, *"It is Finished."* This is the *Spirit of Truth* speaking about the cup. The Spirit of Truth makes absolute declarations that cannot be altered. Most of the time when the Spirit of Truth is speaking it is quite simple, authoritative and cutting. The picture of the Spirit of truth is the double-edged sword in Jesus' mouth in Revelation 1:16. Truth cannot be debated, but may get us hated. Truth speaking will either cause us to be hated or celebrated. When Jesus said, *"into your hands I commit my spirit"* he then offered up his life or Spirit. This was the *Spirit of Life* speaking. This is rather brief description of something that is deeper than I fully understand. I hope the fullness of the Spirit upon Christ stirs a deep hunger in you to seek him like never before.

Important Scriptures to meditate upon:

The Spirit of Burning and Judgment (Isaiah 4:4)

The Spirit of Intercession or Grace and Supplications (Romans 8:27 and Zechariah 12:10)

The Spirit of Life (Romans 8:2 and Romans 8:10)

The Spirit of Truth (John 14:17 and John 15:26 and John 16:13)

The Spirit of Holiness (Romans 1:4 and 2 Corinthians 7:1)

The Spirit of Adoption (Romans 8:15 and Romans 8:23)

The Spirit of Prophecy (Revelation 19:10)

Chapter 8
The Five Wise Virgins

Many people saw Jesus hanging on the cross from a distance, but those who were close to Him while He was on it found their identity in the Crucified Lord of Glory. Seeing from a distance, versus seeing up close and personal is very different. Seeing Jesus from a distance did not necessarily identify the person with the one on the cross. Being at the foot of the cross clearly identified those who were there as his most devoted followers. All four Gospels have an account of Jesus speaking from the cross. However the Gospel of John is the only Gospel where the writer is at the foot of the cross. *John 19: 25 "Now there stood by the Cross of Jesus His Mother, and His Mother's sister, Mary the wife of Cleophas, and Mary Magdalene."* This is John speaking and the very next two verses Jesus speaks to His Mother and to His brother. Jesus said that those who do the will of my Father are my mother and Brother. So being at the foot of the Cross was the Father's will. He had to forsake His Son, but it was still His will for John to be there. The Father was pleased with the Son but had to look away from him when he became sin. Then he poured out the Cup of His Wrath upon him. Jesus didn't just become sin; all of the wrath that was to eternally punish sin came upon Jesus. Could you imagine seeing Jesus while He was drinking the Wrath of God? These Five wise virgins did, for they went out to meet the Bridegroom in the midnight hour, as He was laying His life down for His Bride. The five wise virgins parable in action is these five wise ones who went out to meet the Bridegroom. Parables are mysteries, but they are actions also. For example, the parable of the vineyard is Jesus being crucified or killed by the religious world. Another would be the Merchant who buys the pearl, Jesus would be the Merchant, you and I would be the pearl, and His precious blood would be the price. These five saw Jesus drinking the cup while he was on the Cross; to me this is beautiful and terrifying just like the Man on the Cross.

Scripture gives some awesome word pictures of how John very closely related to Jesus. One time Peter, who walked on water with Jesus, asked John to ask Jesus a question. The question I have is why would Peter ask such a question through John, Peter was a man who received revelation from the Father in Heaven, Peter walked on water. The reason he asked John to ask Jesus is because Peter perceived that John so positioned himself before the Lord that he knew how to receive from Jesus. If you can't receive from Jesus, you can never give to Him or to others. Here is a picture of how John positioned Himself before Jesus. *John 13:23-24 "Now there was leaning on Jesus' bosom one of His disciples, who Jesus loved. Simon Peter therefore beckoned him, that he should ask who it should be whom he spoke."* Jesus responds to them, Judas dips in the sop and took communion in unworthily fashion. Be careful with what you do to the body of Christ, and with His blood! The person who Jesus responds to is the one who laid down, who trust's in Him, who's not ashamed of Him, and whose ear is ready to hear. Jesus came from the bosom of the Father and now John's lying on the bosom of the Son, what a marvelous privilege to not be ashamed to love Jesus like that. John was no closet Christian. John also out ran Peter to the tomb after Jesus' resurrection in John 20:4. *Love always will out run zeal.* Peter loved Jesus more than the rest, but he had to grow into that love and

Jesus said that to Peter after he had received forgiveness for lying to Jesus by saying He wouldn't deny him. Forgiveness is what frees us to Love God. The cross is the single most powerful act of love ever. Also if John would have totally been asleep in the garden when Jesus prayed, perhaps we would not have had access possibly to the greatest prayer ever prayed in John 17? This is a brief picture of John carrying His cross before and after while Jesus was on His. John's deepest desire was Jesus, and that desire brought Him to the foot of the cross. Many years later John sees Jesus glorified, on the island of Patmos, as a slain Lamb still bearing the wounds that John watched him acquire. Jesus still wasn't done revealing Himself. In the book of Revelation Jesus continues to reveal himself to John. Truly Jesus was John's exceedingly great reward.

Now let us see the character of someone who gave birth to the Son of God. Mary didn't only give birth to the Son of God. She also gave birth to the perfect will of God and risked her very life to do it. According to the Law she could have been stoned for being pregnant and not married. If Joseph were having a bad hair day, perhaps he would have stoned her? Impossible. Why? Because Jesus was Lord in the womb, just ask Elizabeth, see Luke 1:43.

Idolaters pray to Mary, wise people learn from those who give birth to the purposes of God, not pray to them. Mary didn't only know how to respond to the Word of the Lord, she knew how to receive it and therefore she could give birth to it or Him. She responds in a simple way to probably one of the most profound miracles ever. Mary may have been blessed and highly favored but she was just as human as the rest of us and she too needed a savior. Now you have a chosen woman favored of God, but still a sinner who will give birth to the only sinless flesh ever to live, the devil had nothing in Him. Only God could pull that one off. When the Angel Gabriel who stands in the presence of the Lord came to her she responded in a way that no one else would have, which may be why God chose her. Mary had no reference point for it had never been done before, nor would it be ever done again, and because of this Virgin birth men and women could be born again.

Let's look at her response to the word of the Lord that came from the Angel. When God sends an Angel it is so men do not get glory, every time you see an Angel sent from God there is a specific reason why. *Luke 1:38 KJV "And Mary said, Behold the handmaid of the Lord; be it unto me according to thy word. And the Angel departed from her."* The Angel Gabriel came prophesying to her, she simply received it. She didn't worry or fear the possibility of her being stoned; she could have said, "What will people think? What about the religious people who don't know how to interpret prophecy? They may think I am a heretic?" Mary simply believed the word, and we must simply believe before we can receive it and give birth to it. Who she gave birth turned out to be her Savior. That sounds pretty humbling to me. Later Jesus became subject to Joseph and Mary's authority. This is the Creator and Savoir becoming subject to His very creation. Even Jesus submitted to authority. Jesus always displays perfect love and humility in everything he says and does.

As a boy Jesus was in the temple astonishing the religious leaders of his day with His understanding and answers. Then Mary and Joseph came telling him they were seeking Him sorrowing, wondering what happened to him. They were obviously worried, yet Jesus makes no apology for them getting ahead of God. Rather He tells them He must be About His Fathers Business. Even as a boy Jesus was confident about his identity as God's Son. His earthly Father and mother come to him worried and he responds to his natural Father and mother, *"I must be about my fathers business."* His earthly Father was a carpenter. Imagine the insecurity they felt when Jesus said that. Joseph and Mary didn't understand what Jesus said, but His mother kept all these sayings in her heart. She was abiding in Christ and his words were abiding in her. When we abide in Christ we can stand in adversity, because greater is he who is in us than he that is in the world. Mary wound up at the foot of the cross. The Word of God abiding in her brought her to the cross, Her response to the Angel's prophecy allowed her to give birth to her savior and Lord.

How we handle the Word of God is what will determine how we treat the Cross of Jesus Christ. The Words came from heaven on to a page written by men. The pages came from a Tree that died with living words on them. The Man from heaven came and was hung on a dead tree by men. However how we obey the Scriptures to show how much we value his blood that was shed. It is pretty interesting that Jesus' words are written in red in most Bibles. If we abide in Him and His words abide in us we will you be at the foot of His Cross. Meaning when the pressure is on we will not deny the Lord who bought us. The Living abiding Word of God abode in Mary bringing her where the Lord of Glory was crucified and pierced so she could be pierced also. *Jesus had to die to live the prophetic word over his life. So it is with us.* I personally believe that while Jesus was being pierced, his mother Mary was receiving the prophetic word over her life that she received from Simeon. *Luke 2:34-35 KJV "And Simeon blessed them, and said unto Mary his mother, Behold, this child is set for the fall and rising again of many in Israel; and for a sign which shall be spoken against; (Yea, a sword shall pierce through thy own soul also,) that the thoughts of many hearts may be revealed."* Jesus is dying to live out the word over his life. That word was coming alive in Mary as her soul was being pierced through the suffering of her Son. This piercing was so that *"the thoughts of many would be revealed."* The thoughts of many being revealed, is speaking of true prophetic ministry. There is a lesson in this for us. When we live out the word over our life, it opens the door for others to step into their destiny and live out the word of God over their lives.

There is not much in Scripture about Mary's sister. However she is certainly known in heaven for her dedication to the Son of God. She publicly was not ashamed of Him. There was a risk and danger involved in being at the foot of His Cross. Now we would call it guilty by association. For scripture not to say much about a person it is actually saying something. In the Old Testament when a Prophet would come to Israel, like in Judges 6:8, with no name there's a message behind that. It is that the name is irrelevant; the message is where the relevancy is found. It takes all the focus off the person and puts all the focus on their actions or words at the time when they are mentioned. Similar to this woman, she's not spoken about nearly half as much as Judas and he betrayed Jesus. She was not ashamed of Him and she had the privilege of being close to him and hearing his voice before he offered himself for her. There are only a very few people in all of eternity who heard Jesus' voice during that time and she is one of the five. Since she showed up at the cross we should honor her willingness to risk for loves' sake.

Scripture also doesn't have a lot to say of the wife of Cleophas. However keep in mind she is one of five wise virgins who is the midnight hour or the hour of darkness and adversity stood with the Lord. This woman was with a company of valiant and courageous lovers of the Lord Jesus Christ. They were willing to be identified with Him in His death. This is a picture of the chosen, those who were making their calling and election sure, those who were walking out their salvation with fear and trembling. If we hang out with wise men we will become wise. Remember birds of a feather flock together. Hang out with dogs and you will get flees.

Hang out with cowards and you will compromise, for compromise is the action of a coward.

This company at the cross had no mixed interests, Jesus was everything to them and it was visible to the outside world. Their light was set on a hill literally that day at the hill of Golgotha. While darkness covered the earth, their light in the Spirit was shinning. Truly their light did shine before men. Just imagine the delight of the Father over those 5 people who stood and beheld the Lamb of God while he was taking away the sins of the world. Imagine the pain in the Father's heart. He had to crush His Well Beloved Son, who was innocent. The Father poured the cup of wrath on His Son. The Father had to forsake His Son while He was on the Cross. Meanwhile these 5 wise virgins stood with Him. The Father lifted His presence from the Son because the Son could only do what He saw the Father do. He then offered His breath. After all that was written was fulfilled. I could imagine the Father looking away from the Son, all of Heaven silent in awe of the Father's grief and pain while His emotions are filling heaven's atmosphere. All of Heaven was being touched with the Sacrifice of his Precious Son. While these five wise virgins have their eyes intently fixed on Jesus, the Roman soldier pierces His side and everything that Jesus is, is poured out for those who are undeserving of His Kindness.

Just for a second feel the Father's heart for this company at the cross and also the man who helped Jesus carry His cross. Ask the Holy Spirit to let your heart feel this truth like never before. Imagine the place they have in the Son's heart as they heard the unspoken cry and longing of the Father's heart, *"who will stand with my Son when I can't?"* Lets step into the word and feel what is happening. Let Jesus' sacrifice tenderize our hearts enough to change our minds and make us live differently.

Mary Magdalene also was part of this company. This woman once had seven devils in her that Jesus cast out, see Luke 8:2. Some think of Mary Magdalene as an embodiment of Israel. Israel had seven demonic nations that they never fully conquered. *Deuteronomy 7:1 KJV "When the LORD thy God shall bring thee into the land whither thou goest to possess it, and hath cast out many nations before thee, the Hittites, and the Girgashites, and the Amorites, and the Canaanites, and the Perizzites, and the Hivites, and the Jebusites, seven nations greater and mightier than thou;"* These nations were never fully wiped out, and the principalities still contend for the Covenant people of God in the New Testament. These principalities seek to hinder God's people from his promises.

After Mary Magdalene was set free by the truth, who is a person, she was changed forever. Truth is eternal therefore the change it brings is forever if we hold fast. Mary Magdalene went from having seven demons in her to being at the foot of the cross. *Luke 7:47 KJV "Wherefore I say unto thee, Her sins, which are many, are forgiven; for she loved much: but to whom little is forgiven, the same loveth little."* This verse perfectly describes the story of her life. She was also at the tomb for Jesus' resurrection right before his ascension. How is that for timing? Often those who are hungry for God discern the times and seasons. Jesus said to her "touch me not; for I have not ascended to the Father." Perhaps here we see the Father's and the Son's passion for one another. No one could touch Jesus until they had a family reunion in Heaven. The Holy Spirit raised Jesus from the dead and they were off to see the Father, but not until Mary Magdalene received a word from Jesus. He told her to tell His friends, His brethren what He was doing. Jesus loves to tell His people what He's doing and He chooses to use people it will be hard to receive from to see if we are humble or proud. This woman was forever ruined by what Jesus had done for her on the cross is why she showed up at the tomb. This was a woman who really received a touch from the Lord Jesus and was forever grateful. The scary part to me is that there were four women and one man at the foot of the cross. This is similar to prayer meetings today. The ratio of women to men is still like four to one, this is not acceptable, and it is changing in Jesus name. Men must rise up and be courageous like the second Adam, not passive like the first Adam. If Jesus was courageous and humble enough to go through a terribly painful, shameful and horrific death for us perhaps we can show up and stand up for him.

This company at the cross is famous in Heaven and their character should be noticed and learned from. They were not afraid to risk their life while Jesus was giving His. They were co-laboring with Him in His weakest hour and this truly must have brought the Father to tears. If any human being ever did one single thing right this must have been it. They could not have done this if it weren't for Grace. Remember Grace helps us to stand for Truth and they did right by the foot of His cross. Mercy was for those disciples who didn't show up at the Cross. Mercy picks us up when we fall and Grace helps us to stand in the Truth. We should learn from these five wise virgins who hade oil in their lamb in the hour of adversity. They went out to meet the Bridegroom as He was purchasing them. It so good to be His property, you are God's greatest investment; he gave His precious Son for you. Jesus believes in you a lot more than an insecure religious leader. He believes in you way more than you believe in yourself. When Jesus said from the cross, "it is finished" he meant it. *Philippians 1:6 KJV "Being confident of this very thing, that he which hath begun a good work in you will perform it until the day of Jesus Christ:"* Perhaps Paul's confidence toward the Philippians was rooted in what Jesus said from Calvary? I to am confident that Jesus who is the Author and the Finisher will finish the work he has began in your life.

Chapter 9
The offense of the cross

The cross will offend everyone who does not get on it. We will either be offended or crucified, one or the other. Being Crucified with Christ will keep us from being offended by the cross and God's unchanging truth. The cross is everything humanity doesn't want, but it actually everything we need. We need to be dead to sin and alive to God. Only after humanity is crucified will Jesus will send the Holy Spirit to us. Then deity will live in humanity making us a temple of Holy Spirit. We become partakers of the divine nature when God sends his Precious Holy Spirit to us. The cross of Jesus is the very wisdom God. The Wisdom of God builds people and things that endure the fire of testing and the storm of adversity for the Glory of God. The book of Galatians has a lot to say about the cross. *Galatians 6:17 KJV "From henceforth let no man trouble me: for I bear in my body the marks of the Lord Jesus."* I guess because the cross marked the writer of Galatians he may have some insight into it. Paul speaks about the *offense of the cross*, and it is so real. He also spoke about the *enemies of the Cross*. These are harsh realities that aren't spoken about much but must be understood. It is possible to preach the cross and be an enemy of it. The life of the cross is death to self. The offense of the cross will cause us to be persecuted, or called narrow minded. Others will call us arrogant for saying there is only one way, and his name is Jesus. When these things are being said about us it is because we are carrying our cross denying ourselves, and the life of Christ is being made manifest in and through us. The offense of the cross is this, anyone who has not got on it will be judged by it. Every sin and wicked thing was paid for by the Lord Jesus on His Cross, which is why we must meet Him on His and be sure to carry ours. The Cross confronts every sin, every religious Spirit, every imperfection of mankind's flesh, and fully redeems anyone who will receive Jesus Christ, follow Him and obey Him. That is good news that should give us joy unspeakable.

Jesus fulfilled the Law, drank the cup for those who did not fulfill the law, making circumcision unnecessary to be righteous or clean. Jesus made us clean by the shedding of His very own blood. This was causing controversy; it was like a religious spirit was demanding circumcision to be necessary. This was happening when Paul wrote the book of Galatians. When Jesus' sacrifice made the circumcision of the heart possible for Jew and Gentile alike. Religion always put great precedence on what man does. Meaning we become clean because of circumcision. Religion always puts the focus on man. The truth is that we put our trust in Christ's accomplishment and then we start to become like the one we have put our trust in. There were religious men who didn't want to be persecuted for the cross. So they came up with a solution "you must be circumcised." Religion says *you must,* Jesus said *"It is finished".* Learning to live in what Jesus has said and done is how we abide in him, this happens when his word abides in us. His word keeps us from sin and also leads us in the way we should go.

Jesus wants to kill us, hence "take up your cross and follow Me." This is so we won't be offended. We will either carry the cross or be offended by it. *The Cross of Jesus makes every other religion a lie, that is very offensive in a world where everyone wants to be his or her own god.* There is even a false teaching that states Jesus had to become God, or that Jesus was born again. Jesus was God from before the foundation of the world; he always was and will always be God. A bad translation of the Bible teaches that he couldn't grasp being equal with God. *Philippians 2:6 NIV "Who, being in the very nature of God, did not consider equality with God something to be grasped."* This is a bad translation, especially when Jesus said in John 8:58 to the Jew *"Before Abraham was I am."* Jesus obviously grasped or understood who he was. This translation is insulting to the person of Christ. The more Christ friendly translation reads *Philippians 2:6 KJV "Who, being in the form of God, thought it not robbery to be equal with God:"* This translation is a lot more congruent with Christ's own words in John 8:58. Jesus was God in the womb thus Elizabeth said to Mary *"the mother of my Lord has come to me."* Jesus was in the womb and was Lord, this is further proven when the Gospel of Matthew say *"he was born King of the Jews."* (See Luke 1:43, Matthew 2:2)

John 15:13 "Greater love has no man than this, that a man lay down his life for his friends." On the very implement Jesus laid down His life for His friends, also makes enemies. There are enemies of the cross, whose God is their belly, who mind earthly things, whose end is destruction. Paul said, *"am I your enemy because I tell you the Truth."* Not only does the cross make enemies, so does the man Christ Jesus who died on it. The Truth makes us free, so why would people want to be in opposition to their own freedom? What Jesus did on the cross saves our life, why be in opposition to the one man who did something for everyone and only wants us in return? Being an enemy of the cross is rather foolish, for everyone who met a cross was conquered by it. It is 100% successful in putting anyone to death, painfully and slowly. The cross is something we want to come in agreement with and meet Jesus on, so we may have life and have it more abundantly. Jesus is called the *stone of stumbling and a rock of offense*, it deeply bothers the Father if people trip over the one who laid down His life for them. Sometimes Christians are called judgmental and sometimes they are. However there are other times where a Christian is carrying a cross near someone who is bound in sin. That cross they are carrying (prophetically speaking of a completely obedient life) carries the judgment of that sin, and a victory proclamation over that sin. Many times the person bound and blinded by sin doesn't see the victory proclamation that is nailed to the cross as an invitation. *The cross is an invitation to the abundant life Christ promised. Only Jesus can make a pagan implement of death by capital punishment, an invitation to Eternal life and pay our way to heaven on it!* Everything about Jesus is supernatural, he is better than we think, which is why he gave us his mind.

Before Jesus went to the cross, someone was offended by the working of it. The cross stretches us unto a broken heart as it did to Jesus. A broken hearted person's life exposes a hard-hearted person without even trying. The same way one's true Biblical faith in action naturally attacks or exposes someone else's unbelief or complacency. When Mary anointed Jesus at Bethany she was weeping, and wiping his feet with her hair. The hair of a women is her glory according to 1 Corinthians 11:15. So she's taking what is known as her glory, and wiping it on the dirtiest part of a human that was exposed, his feet. Feet were dirty because they wore sandals and walked on dusty roads. Jesus' dirty feet were so worthy even of this women's glory, she publicly did this. She anointed Him for burial; through her brokenness she perceived what was next for Jesus. She could prophetically see exactly what was the will of the Father for Christ and she partnered with it. She obviously knew something no one else on the face of the earth knew, this is why she broke the Alabaster Box open and anointed Him. If His disciples were on point and on the same page as Him, they would have emptied out the treasury and bought the oil and did it. This woman foresaw the cross in Jesus' very near future, and wherever the Gospel goes, so goes her story. Jesus could have told the story of Peter walking on Water or of Moses parting the red sea, yet God chose her love offering to be directly attached to the gospel. This woman is everything the Father looks for in a worshipper. She was broken over her sin, her offering was very costly, and it was public. While her physical position was the lowest one in the room, at Jesus' feet, she received the highest honor, more than anyone else in the history of mankind. For everywhere the Gospel goes there her testimony must be told. Everywhere in the Greek means "everywhere." Jesus has seen a lot of great testimonies, but this was the one He chose to be attached to the Gospel. Prophetically this woman knew what was ahead for Jesus and she blessed it, and became a part of what God was doing.

This was one of the only encouragements Jesus received to continue to fulfill the Father's will. Peter didn't want Him to die, His disciples didn't want to hear about His sufferings, but this woman saw the purposes of God and spent all on them. This Alabaster oil was costly; her offering that only came from the working of the cross in her own life, unto a broken heart. This act of worship even offended Judas the betrayer. The Gospel of Luke tells us this woman was a sinner. The Pharisee went out of his way to say that she was unclean. The offense of the cross was manifested even before the cross, while Jesus was being anointed for burial or death. The offense of the cross-targeted two people. One being Judas the Betrayer who betrayed Jesus for thirty pieces of Silver, the other being Simon the Pharisee who was questioning Jesus' discernment. The offense the cross will manifest clearly in those who love money and those who are of a religious spirit, notice the Cross offended both of them. This broken hearted worship offended a hard-hearted religious man, and a deceitfully wicked betrayer. They were not offended by her profound sermon, but her fragrant worship. The fact that she was willing to spend herself on the one who would spend Himself on her, and the world in whom God loved so much he sent Jesus. According to the religious perspective of the Pharisee this woman was a sinner and was unclean. Let's say he was right, there is a possibility she literally sold her very self to attain that oil and so she knew what it felt like to be paid for. She had been paid for by evildoers and Jesus was about to pay for evildoers. This woman did not give something that did not cost her something. However she attained that precious oil; she spent it in the right place. Judas was concerned about the money, the religious man was concerned that Jesus didn't know who was touching him, and they both should have been more concerned with touching Jesus and keeping their eyes on him. Judas should have been less concerned with money that was not his. Remember the enemies of the cross *"mind earthly things"*. When we lose focus we are then positioning ourselves for our values to be altered. Simon the Pharisee was focused on "what Jesus supposedly wasn't discerning about this sinful woman." Judas the betrayer was focusing on "what could have been done with the money or that he could have stolen the money." They were both focused on what wasn't happening instead of the great exploit that was happening. They were seeing the will of God from a human perspective and they were enemies of the cross. Simon the Pharisee and Judas both had something in common they were offended. *Often offense comes when people live from the wrong perspective, some would call it deception.* They were offended because of this broken woman's prophetic insight, in that she could see the cross. Their offense led to a mild persecution of this woman. Offense blinds someone spiritually. Judas thought he knew how better to spend the money then on Jesus, and Simon the Pharisee, according to his lofty opinion, thought he could see her spiritual condition a little more clearly than Jesus. This doesn't sound like you or I. We would never think or dare verbalize such insulting things to Jesus. We have never been blind to what God is doing do to our own agenda or offense, or have we?

Mary was aware of how badly her past offended Jesus, which is what caused her tears and the abandoned worship. Remember *"Godly sorrow works repentance."* Unfortunately these men were more concerned with teaching Jesus how to be God. Remember God doesn't need help being God; he is God all by himself. God resists the proud, but he exalts the humble. *If God is not exalting us perhaps we are not as humble as we think we are.* This woman's humility got her testimony forever attached to the Gospel. Not bad, huh? I am almost nervous to preach the Gospel without sharing about Jesus being anointed first. The offense the cross leads to the persecution the cross brings. This happened even before Jesus went to the cross because he was the Lamb Slain from before the foundation of the world. The offense and the persecution of the cross are seen in the book of Genesis. The offense came over worship again when Abel offered a Lamb the only acceptable sacrifice, leading to him being the first Martyr of the Lord Jesus. Cain killed Abel because of the Offense of the Cross; Jesus dying on the cross is the only sacrifice that pleases God. Abel was not only persecuted he was murdered or martyred. Truth is eternal and the carnal mind cannot distinguish what Truth is, for Truth is a person in Jesus and a Spirit that is Holy.

Persecution comes in different levels; it could be slander, false accusations, slow torture or even martyrdom. Persecution comes from those who don't see through God's eyes, it comes to all those who will live Godly in Christ Jesus. Judas and Simon the Pharisee weren't going to martyr her in the flesh with Jesus standing there obviously, but they couldn't discern true worship. It is clear how they responded that they were not seeing from a God's perspective. The carnal mind is truly in enmity with God, it is not only enmity with God but it is also at enmity with what he is doing. Persecution also is someone responding the wrong way when something right has been done. Jesus taught us to always respond to persecution in the opposite Spirit. That is denying yourself and taking up your cross. Blessing for cursing, becoming an advocate for your false accuser before the throne. This is learned from Jesus' teaching in Luke 6, and in what he displayed on the cross when he asked the Father to forgive those who tortured, mocked Him and nailed Him to a tree and were not apologizing for it.

What Jesus taught from the Cross is what we boldly approach the throne through and with. If we pursue Jesus with a cross, He will pursue us with a Throne. The Throne is unapproachable without the cross; one can never come before the throne unless we have come through the veil of His flesh. If God so chooses to pursue you with a Throne as He did Ezekiel, just fall down and worship him. Remember the Kingdom can come because the King came to earth to die for us that we may become citizens of his Kingdom. The Kingdom comes because the throne has wheels, see Ezekiel 1: 16-19 to know I am not a heretic.

God does whatever He wants, he does what he pleases. Any words that try to describe God are an eternal understatement, that's why for eternity to eternity we will bow before the Lamb and He will be our light forever and ever. Meaning it will take forever to reveal all that he is. There is a progression of the cross in the book of Galatians; it goes from *the offense of the cross*, to *the persecution of the cross*, to *the marks of the cross*, and then to *the boasting of the cross*. We by grace will touch on the marks of the cross next.

Chapter 10
The marks of the cross

There is no way we can carry the cross and not be marked by it. The cross forever marked Jesus. Paul also was literally marked by the cross. There is a vast difference between Paul's marks and Jesus'. However if you saw Paul's back and Jesus' you would not know who's who. Paul's back was opened up 5 times, for he received thirty-nine lashes five times. *2 Corinthians 11:24 KJV "Of the Jews five times received I forty stripes save one."* Remember religion is very painful. He had wounds on top of wounds. However Paul's marks were from his scars of service, and Jesus' are for our proof of purchase. Our God and King, who spent Himself on us, will always wear sin's paid debt on his physical body. There is no one like Jesus period, that's part of my statement of Faith.

In this we will be marked, either by the cross or the beast. We will either overcome by the Blood of the Lamb and the word of our testimony, and not loving your life even unto death. Or be marked by the beast and destined for the lake of fire, stored up for the devil and his angels. No person bearing the image of God was designed for hell, that's why Jesus paid such a high price for our ransom. The truth is offensive as is the cross, which leads to the persecution of the cross, then comes the marks of the cross. The mark of the beast is the point of no return as are the marks of the cross. Paul became so intimately acquainted with the Lord Jesus, through the fellowship of his sufferings, that he didn't even want to live on this planet any longer. Paul had been marked by the cross so deeply that he said *to die is gain,* meaning he was ready to go where the cross of Jesus gained him eternal access to. When someone bears the marks of the cross, it is because they have been crucified with Christ, carried the cross, preached the cross, and have been persecuted for it. The *marks or stigma* in Greek literally means, *scar of service or the recognition of ownership.* The marks on Paul's back validated Jesus' proof of purchase. For Jesus owned Paul, for he purchased him with His very own Blood, and Paul's physical body verified this purchase by bearing on his body the *"recognition of ownership."* This truth gives this verse great expression. *1 Corinthians 6:20 KJV "For ye are bought with a price: therefore glorify God in your body, and in your spirit, which are God's."*

Not every Christian will have literal marks on their physical body, but the working of the cross leaves the marks of the cross. It is our lifestyle that proves Christ has bought us and we are His. For some it may be literal marks and physical persecution, for others it may not go that far. Some may be martyred some may not, let the will of God be done. Remember God doesn't give anyone more than they can handle. The marks of the cross also show the world that it is crucified to you; the world can see those marks on you and know you are not of them. If we are crucified with Christ, the flesh and lusts of it are also dead to us. Meaning that the things that used to tempt us are no longer appealing to us. It would be hard to tempt a dead man; it also would be hard to offend a dead man. We are Christ's property; he owns us and has marked us in the Spirit with what marked him in the flesh. The roman soldier that whipped Jesus was born to do so. Those wounds are forever. One day, the antichrist will try to mark everyone on this planet, and only those who bear the marks of the cross shall be able to resist this evil that is coming, Revelation 19:20.

We can't even get to the cross by ourselves; we need someone to help us carry it when we can no longer do so. We will learn to love as Jesus loves. In this we will learn to prefer one another, that is the life of the cross, it is seen in our relationships with one another. I prefer you and you prefer me, and men know whose we are by how we love. When you can no longer carry your cross, the enemy tries to release condemnation but God sends grace in the area of the person of the Holy Spirit or even a real natural person to help you carry your cross. This is so death can be swiftly executed. Grace allows you to fulfill the purposes of God, and those purposes of God have all to do with the cross and being marked by it. *Galatians 6:17 "From henceforth let no man trouble me: for I bear on my body the marks of the Lord Jesus."* This is a profound statement by Paul the Apostle. He didn't want to play religious games because the cross had marked him. *When the cross marks a person they will have no interest in playing religious games.* Men and women of old who were marked by the cross, died so that we could have the Word of God. If we only read the word we will gain knowledge that puffs up, but if we eat it the word will become flesh and we will have revelation from the Author himself causing us to lay down our life just as he did. The cross is the only place of being elevated, but humbled at the same time, or being high, but laying down, all at one time. The cross is the only place where you can taste life and death in one cup. There is a tension the cross brings like nothing else ever. Being marked by the cross causes us to move on past the he said, she said, nominal and irrelevant circumstances that arise in modern Christianity. It seemed that the marks on Paul's back were more relevant then the troublesome situations he was telling people to no longer bother him with. Most of those situations are not profitable and waste tons of time and energy anyway. Most of Christian's problems come from looking from different perspectives at the same person or circumstances. The solution is the cross, and being suspended on it until we see from his perspective. In death we can really see from the perspective of eternal life. Which is why we have been given the mind of Christ, so that we can see from God's perspective. The cross allows us to be lifted up but permits us from being proud.

The marks of the cross will absolutely change our priorities, and even our vision. When we our marked by His cross, we are counted among the faithful. All through the ages, faithful men and woman have endured torture, persecution and all kinds of tribulation so that the unsearchable riches of Christ can be preached. From the beginning of the church age, the cross has burned in the hearts of the faithful men and women. Not only has it burned in their hearts, some of their physical bodies have been marked by it as well, for this I am truly grateful. I have a special love for all those whose lives proclaim, "Worthy is the Lamb is the Lamb that was slain" and have suffered for His name's sake. I would rather spend time with a Christian who has been marked by the cross, then one who has success according to the world's standards.

The cross doesn't just mark the backs and bodies of the faithful, it marks time itself. The demarcation of time that the cross of Christ brings to the humanity is a fascinating topic. The atheist, muslim, catholic, mormon, or any other false religion still has to operate in the time the cross has marked. The time line of human History was, has, and always will be marked, by a man who was fully God, and fully man who went to the cross offered up His life died. He rose again on the third day, to purchase us out of every, tribe, kindred and nation. We live in A.D., which is commonly known as "after death", but in Latin it is "Anno Domine" which translated means "the year of the Lord." The coming of Jesus on the earth as flesh has marked and divided the time frame of all of humanity through out the ages. The purpose of Jesus' life in the flesh on earth was to come and die for us so that we may live in the "year of the Lord" for ages until his return.

In Daniel 7:25 it speaks of the antichrist who will try to change time and laws. I believe this is an assault on Jesus and the cross, because the cross of Jesus validated Jesus' dominion to mark time, and this beast wants to mark men and deny that Jesus came by changing times and seasons. The accuser of the brethren tries similar tactics with His words. Which is why he is called the accuser of the brethren. The devil tries to bring up the past and tries to uncover what the blood has covered. He likes to swim in the sea of forgetfulness and he brings things to our memory that God has chosen to forgive, which means he forgets. The enemy wants to remind us of what the blood covers, because it doesn't cover him. The enemy will not bring up something we need to repent of because He can never repent, for he is already judged. The accuser will bring up what we have repented of so as to bring us condemnation by trying to deceive us into not believing we are truly forgiven. The enemy hates healing because he can never be healed; he hates the cross for his head was bruised when Jesus' heels were bruised as his feet were nailed to the tree. The cross marks the time he is limited to until he meets the lake of fire for all of eternity. Time can be redeemed because it is measured by the redeemer himself. Satan hates the Gospel for it is God's time schedule on when his end will be. *Matthew 24:14 KJV "And this gospel of the kingdom shall be preached in all the world for a witness unto all nations; and then shall the end come."* He hates the Gospel because it redeems time, and he is unredeemable, and his days are numbered.

The cross does not only mark the faithful and time itself it also marks God Himself. The Father forever will remember what He allowed to be done to His dear and precious Son for us because of His abundant love, which was towards us through the veil of his

Son's flesh. The marks that Paul bore on his body were the marks of Jesus Christ. The marks of the cross are the very signature of Jesus on a human life. All of us need the signature of the great author and finisher on our lives. His approval is necessary for our success, and suffering is simply part of God's equation that adds up to Christ being formed in us. He should always be on our mind, for we are always on His. We were the joy set before him. Christ endured the cross so that we would endure to the end and faithfully finish the race we are running as we look unto Jesus.

Chapter 11
When you can no longer carry your cross

John 19:16-17 "Then delivered he him therefore unto them to be crucified. And they took Jesus and led him away. And he bearing his cross went forth into the place of a skull, which in the Hebrew Golgotha:"

Here we see the deliver being delivered to deliver us from death and hell. The place of the skull is the place where Abraham built an Altar to the Lord. It was there where Isaac got saved at an altar call, when the Angel of the Lord called from heaven to Abraham, Genesis 22:11. A Lamb was sent to take Isaac's place, but no one was sent to take Jesus' place. This is the place where the Lord appeared to David. Here is where Solomon built the temple to the Lord. This was a familiar place to Jesus; his glory once rested in the temple made with hands, and is now soon to leave the temple of His body as he approaches the place of the skull. This account of the Gospel shows Jesus carrying His cross, clearly. There are three other accounts where a man named Simon a Cyrenian, is compelled by the Roman soldiers to carry Jesus' cross. The Romans were used to crucifying people, they did it as a job. Somewhere between Jesus carrying the cross and Simon carrying the cross, Jesus had a breaking point. Jesus at this time was fully God and fully man, and he could grasp equality with God for he was God. Jesus at this point humbled himself and put his divine attributes on the shelf, still being God but not relying on his divine attributes. He walked on water, he could have made the cross hover over his head and flexed the muscle of His Divinity, but rather he chose to glorify God in His flesh and be weak. God cannot be beat into submission. Some people think they can pray God into submitting to their own will but this is not true either. Jesus chose this; he modeled full surrender to the Father no matter what it would cost him. He modeled for us that the flesh is merely for a sacrifice. The ultimate Humility was shown as He became obedient to the death of the cross. Christ's supremacy is seen in his complete humility and surrender to the will of his Father. We look at supreme as in charge, but God has put his Son Jesus in charge because of his surrender. It is the Father that gave Jesus a highly exalted name. The way to be exalted in the kingdom is to humble yourself. Jesus humbled himself to the death of a cross and the Father gave him a highly exalted name. The way up in the Kingdom is down.

Jesus' humanity was beat to the point where he could no longer carry the cross. His deity had decided to purchase all of humanity back to God on it. We can't even get to the cross ourselves; we need someone to help us carry it when we no longer can. The grace of God not only saves but also gives us grace to even come to the place of death alive so we can willingly die. Jesus said, *"no man takes my life but I lay it down."* God desires the same kind of submission from his followers. Mike Bickle said that "God wants' voluntary lovers," and I fully agree with that statement. Some say it takes God to love God and I say it definitely takes God to love your brothers and sisters in Christ, haha. We are saved by Grace through Faith. God puts his grace towards us through Jesus Christ so we can put our faith in him who loved us enough to die for us while we were yet sinners. *James 1:17 KJV "Every good gift and every perfect gift is from above, and cometh down from the Father of lights, with whom is no variableness, neither shadow of turning."* Jesus is the perfect gift and the good gifts the Father gives lead us to the perfect gift. *All signs point to Jesus and all wonders cause us to consider and set our affections on him.* Good gifts are repentance, and healing and others listed in 1 Corinthians 12. The perfect gift is who purchased those gifts for us.

Jesus modeled what he said to Paul in *2 Corinthians 12: 9 KJV "And he said unto me, My grace is sufficient for thee: for my strength is made perfect in weakness. Most gladly therefore will I glory in my infirmities, that the power of Christ may rest upon me."* This verse is seen in action while the weakness of Jesus' human flesh could no longer bear the cross on which he, as God, determined to give His life on. Jesus being fully God, and fully man, all at one time is certainly a great mystery. No one else could have done what Jesus did, for he was the Lamb slain from before the foundation of the world. He alone was capable and worthy to give himself as a ransom for many. Any one who tells you other wise is wrong. Jesus is not a hypocrite, he would not tell you to do something He didn't do or experience, he wanted to reveal the Father because He knew him, for Him and the Father our one. Jesus was touched with our infirmities so much so that he was moved with compassion to heal them. He knows what it feels like to be hungry, thirsty, to feel weak, and to have God's grace upon him, to see that he fulfills the Father's will, Jesus pleased the Father at all costs.

The cross of Jesus is what identifies us with him, and it is where we come through the veil of His flesh and into Him. The holiest of all is a person who is Lord of all. The disciples, who did not show up at the cross, dropped theirs. God grace was sufficient in their weakness just like it is in our weakness. Jesus still came to them after his resurrection, because he didn't know them after the flesh but after the spirit. He didn't relate to them because of their decisions, he related to them based on that the Father had chose them and given them to him. *John 17:24 KJV "Father, I will that they also, whom thou hast given me, be with me where I am; that they may behold my glory, which thou hast given me: for thou lovedst me before the foundation of the world."* The cross is about us being with Jesus where he is.

It is important that we know one another after the Spirit, and not after the flesh. Your flesh and my flesh probably will not get along, but if we know one another after the Spirit we can maintain the unity of the Spirit. This does not mean we agree necessarily on everything, but we are of the same Spirit.

When Jesus called Peter, Jesus had a word of Knowledge for Peter, in that He knew His name before he was even introduced publicly to Peter. Jesus also knew how Peter would walk on water, deny him, and later die for Him. Jesus renamed Him Cephas. This is found in *John 1:42 KJV "And he brought him to Jesus. And when Jesus beheld him, he said thou art Simon the Son of Jona: thou shalt be called Cephas, which is by interpretation, a stone."* When you look at the word "stone" that was used, it means part of a stone. Here Jesus prophetically was saying "Cephas you are a little piece of me, the chief cornerstone." Jesus was calling Him to be a part of His very own body. Somewhere, later down the road, Peter had a revelation of us as living stones. This wasn't just a name it was his calling, and His identity in Christ. Before this could happen Peter had to learn and experience what Jesus said to Paul, *"my grace is sufficient for thee: for my strength is mad perfect in weakness." The only place God's strength can rest is on weakness.* Everything God has ever done is in spite of us and never because of us. The Father loved us enough to send Jesus to find us. We were just like Adam hiding in the garden and He sent His only begotten Son to go find us and bring us home. Jesus had to shed His blood for our dinner ticket to the Marriage Supper.

Peter said to Jesus "I'll die for you," and then denied Him. We often do the very same thing. Say one thing and do another. That may be the definition of hypocrisy. There are many broken relationships in the body of Christ due to this leaven. After Peter denied him, then later he died for him. If we did everything we said we would be the Truth, but we're not and Jesus is and did and that is why we need Him. After Jesus rose from the dead and took back the keys of death and hell, He appeared to His disciples and to the disciple who denied Him three times. Often I have felt just like Peter making a commitment to the Lord and not keeping it, God have mercy on me! In John 21:15-19 Jesus called him Simon three times. It is interesting how Peter or Simon said he would die for Him and another Simon is helping Jesus carry the cross fulfilling Simon Peter's obligation to stand with Jesus in his darkest hour. Three times Jesus calls Peter *"Simon son of Jonas."* What happened? Did Jesus forget that he renamed Him Cephas or Peter? Or was Jesus showing Peter that in spite of you, I chose you. This is rather relieving to someone like me for I identity with Peter in saying I will do something and then not. Still God has graced me with the privilege to feed his sheep. None of you have ever pulled a Peter; you would never do such a thing. Many people read the Bible like how could Peter do that? Like most Christians don't live in the state of Peter's action continually of saying one thing and doing another. There comes a time when we mature in God and move forward into becoming who God says we are, part of his very own body. There comes a time where we start to behave like the Christ who is in us. That is what creation is groaning for and the world around us is hoping for.

Peter's weakness qualified Him. The devil will tell us, that our weakness disqualifies us when it actually qualifies us. Similar to Isaiah, who was a man of unclean lips. So God gets an Angel to get some burning coals from the altar in Heaven and sanctifies what is unclean and uses it to prophesy of His precious Son Jesus. *Religion tries to disqualify us because of our weakness or past, and Jesus says our weakness qualifies us and becomes a landing pad for His power to rest upon us when we confess and repent.* 1 Corinthians 1:26-27 KJV *"For ye see your calling, brethren, how that not many wise men after the flesh, not many mighty, not many noble, are called: But God hath chosen the foolish things of the world to confound the wise; and God hath chosen the weak things of the world to confound the things which are mighty;"* Jesus doesn't only want us to lay on His chest and hear His heart like John the beloved, he also wants to rest upon us. As we learn to rest in Him, he will then in turn rest upon us. Bill Johnson said, *"He is in you for you, and he is upon you for them."* It takes a weak person to learn how to rest in and wait upon God and be still before Him. *Psalm 46:10 KJV "Be still, and know that I am God: I will be exalted among the heathen, I will be exalted in the earth."* In stillness the knowledge of God is released. *We get to know the God we wait upon and search for.* Those who are weak wait upon the Lord and he renews their strength. It is in brokenness and weakness that God changes us. Jacob wrestled with the Angel of the Lord all night, then after the Angel touched his leg and put his hip out of alignment he was named Israel. True Kingdom identity is only released through brokenness and in weakness. *Philippians 3:2 KJV "For we are the circumcision, which worship God in the spirit, and rejoice in Christ Jesus, and have no confidence in the flesh."* After Jacob was crippled he could no longer put confidence in the flesh. Remember everyone in the Kingdom walks with a limp. It was after Peter denied Jesus and became profoundly aware of his weakness, that he could then receive His calling and walk into all that God had for him. Peter was probably a lot more reluctant to put confidence in the flesh after he publicly denied Jesus. *When we become aware of our weaknesses, is when we become a lot more familiar with God's strength.*

Christ was forsaken on His cross, but we are apprehended on ours. When we can no longer carry our cross, it is Jesus who is with us to help us. He has promised to never leave us nor forsake us, that is really good news. It is very humbling to know we can't even take credit for our own death. Often we try to be so spiritual and pious, but the truth is we are in need of God's grace every step of the way. We can't even die to self without his help.

The grace of God turned Peter from being a punk to a hero. He went from being a coward, who trusted in the flesh, to a courageous person, that the Spirit of Glory wrested upon. It is historically accepted that Peter died on a cross upside down. Peter went from running from the cross to dying on one. Scripture reveals that he knew this before hand. *2 Peter 1:14 KJV "Knowing that shortly I must put off this my tabernacle, even as our Lord Jesus Christ hath showed me."* The Lord revealed to him that his time was up, and he was ready to be offered up. Peter went from telling the Lord that he was going to die for him, to receiving from the Lord that he was going to die shortly. We really do live by what God says. God said shortly he would die and he did. God's word released the grace that Peter needed to be willing to die at the hands of the roman government. He went from dropping His cross to dying on one upside down. God sure can do a lot with our weakness if we are willing and obedient. The Holy Spirit changes everything. He gives us power to not love our lives even unto death because Jesus didn't. I am so grateful God calls a man hiding in the wine press, a *"mighty man of Valor"* as he did Gideon. We have been given the mind of Christ so we can see from his perspective. Jesus knocked Paul off his religious high horse and took him down Strait Street blind. Then when Paul received his sight back is when he fully became a new man. We are renewed when we see from God's perspective. The Lord Jesus touches our weakness and brokenness and then glorifies his own name through us when we learn to obey him. God is terribly good. The whole trust in the Lord and lean not on your own understanding thing, is huge. With the foolish and weak things of this world God confounds the wise, which is where you and I come in. It is great to know that we are a part of the Father's plan to glorify his Son Jesus through the Holy Spirit's leading in our lives.

Chapter 12
The prayer of the cross and learning to pray like Christ

According to Scriptures there are three very significant prayers that Jesus prayed. One is the Lord's Prayer also known as the Our Father. This is the prayer in which Jesus taught his disciples to pray. The second prayer of great significance is the prayer before the cross while Jesus was in Garden of Gethsemane. This was fervent prayer like the world has never seen. Jesus literally sweats blood in the place on intercession. The third is the prayer from the cross when Jesus said *"Father forgive them for they know not what they do."* Here Jesus' true selfless nature is shown very clearly. He is hanging there naked and he is asking his Father to forgive people who aren't even asking for it.

To live the Christian life, or rather to die and let Jesus live the Christian life in us, is impossible without prayer being answered. Jesus being on the cross was an answer to His very own prayer as well as the prophecy he inspired the prophets of the Old Testament to prophesy concerning himself. Jesus said to the Father *"Thy will be done"*, and thy will be done put Jesus on a cross and gave Him a cup to drink. Jesus spoke in Mark 10:39 about a cup his followers will drink, and a baptism they will be baptized with. Jesus drank the Cup full of the wrath of God. Jesus tasted death for every man, so we can taste and see that he is good. Human words could never even begin to describe this cup that Jesus drank. The phrase *"Thy will be done"* is seen in three verses which are Matthew 6:10 and Luke 11:2, which is the Lord's Prayer, and also while the Christ was praying in the Garden of Gethsemane in Luke 23:34. Jesus in the garden was not praying about not going to the Cross, for in John 12:32 He said *"And if I be lifted up from the earth, will draw all men unto me."* Jesus in the garden of Gethsemane did not ask not to be lifted up; He asked *"Let this cup pass,* Nevertheless not My will but Thy will be done" and it was as he requested. *Prayer is answered when our request is the Fathers desire.* Before Jesus drank the cup, while He was on the cross, he will was living out the answer of his own prayer. The Lord's Prayer was answered while He was dying on the Cross, He was living in an answer to prayer, which led Him to another prayer, and it was this. *"Father forgive them"* and He did, because Jesus asked Him to. This was one of Jesus' last requests and it was granted. The cross produces a broken heart, which screams *"Father forgive them."*

Jesus would not teach his disciples to pray a prayer that He didn't. Not only did Jesus pray a prayer, but he became the answer to it also. *Prayer that doesn't lead to action is merely verbalized unbelief.* The Lord's Prayer had much to do with the cross that Jesus offered Himself on. *Matthew 6:9-13 KJV "After this manner therefore pray ye: Our Father which art in Heaven, Hallowed be thy name. Thy Kingdom come. Thy will be done in earth as it is in heaven. Give us this day our daily bread. And forgive us our debts, as we forgive our debtors. And lead us not into temptation, but deliver us from evil: for thine are the kingdom, and the power, and the glory forever. Amen."* Jesus teaches His followers to call God "Father" because through the Father's will Jesus would give them power to become sons. *John 1:2 KJV "But as many as received him, to them gave he power to become the sons of God, even to them that believe on his name:"* Through Jesus' full submission to his Father's will we have received power or authority to become sons of God. Which means his Kingdom is our inheritance; there is a place for us in the Father's house prepared just for us by Jesus himself. That is the good news of the Kingdom. The Kingdom of God is within, and it is Righteousness, Peace, and Joy in the Holy Ghost. The shed blood of Jesus attains righteousness for those who believe. Peace is a gift from Jesus paid for by Him being chastised for our Peace. Joy is what caused Jesus to endure the cross. The atmosphere of the Kingdom is the strength of the King, and it is what caused him to endure the cross that he might redeem us to God. All of this is done through the power of the Holy Spirit, the very Spirit that raised Jesus from the dead. It is that same Spirit that will lead us to our cross, and then raise us to new life in Christ Jesus where we are seated with him in heavenly places.

Recently I was in Brooklyn, New York ministering. I had the privilege of eating lunch with an amazing man of God named Rev. Emilio Martinez. He said something that I will never forget. He said this "God leads and satan pushes." This is so true, I hope that blessed you as much as it did me, If not I guess you just had to be there.

Many of Jesus' 12 original disciples literally died on a cross. When Jesus said, *"deny yourself and take up your cross and follow me"* to his disciples this wasn't some figure of speech. This was literal for many of them. Jesus teaches them to pray as he did. *"Thy will be done"* led Jesus to a cross and that is how he teaches his disciples to pray. We were delivered from our own will through Jesus' prayer and obedience. When he said *"Nevertheless not my will, but thy will be done,"* we are delivered from the world through the cross of Christ. Galatians 6:14 KJV *"But God forbid that I should glory, save in the cross of our Lord Jesus Christ, by whom the world is crucified unto me, and I unto the world."* Jesus has fully delivered us, but prayer matures us into the place of radical obedience. *True intimacy with the Lord will always lead to obedience to the Lord and fruitfulness in the Lord.*

Before a seed can be fruitful it must die. Before the palace there is a prison. Before the river there is a wilderness. God in his divine wisdom knows how to order our lives in such a way that he can form his Son Jesus in us. *God knows exactly how to put pressure on us to do something in us.* Christ died for us so that he can live in and through us.

We can learn everything we need to know from Jesus especially when it comes to prayer, for he only did what he saw the Father do and he only said what he heard the Father say. Jesus tells us how and what to pray because he intends to give us what he is telling us to ask for. In Matthew 6 Jesus tells his disciples to pray *"Thy Kingdom come, thy will be done on earth as it is in heaven."* He instructs his disciples to pray in that manner because later he would pray the exact same words. *Matthew 26:42 KJV "He went away again the second time, and prayed, saying, O my Father, if this cup may not pass away from me, except I drink it, **thy will be done**."* The bold phrase is an amazing picture of what the cross does in the life of a believer. The cross is the full surrender of one's will for God's. This is the death that brings forth the abundant, resurrection life that Jesus promises to his followers. *Mark 14:36 KJV "And he said, Abba, Father, all things are possible unto thee; take away this cup from me: nevertheless not what I will, but what thou wilt."* Here we see an interesting word progression that shows us how we as believers mature in intercession. "Abba" is what a young Jewish boy in the days of Jesus would call his Father. "Father" is what a mature son would call his Father. The Abba part of the prayer is "take away this cup from me" the Father part of this prayer is "nevertheless not what I will, but what thou wilt." True prayer is our supplication and our complete surrender. *When a prayer goes from a supplication to a complete surrender it then becomes intercession.* The gap is the place where we stand in the place of obedience.

Matthew 9:36-38 KJV "But when he saw the multitudes, he was moved with compassion on them, because they fainted, and were scattered abroad, as sheep having no shepherd. Then saith he unto his disciples, The harvest truly is plenteous, but the laborers are few; Pray ye therefore the Lord of the harvest, that he will send forth laborers into his harvest." Before the cross we see Jesus tell His disciples to *"pray to the Lord of the Harvest to send forth laborers into His harvest."* It was compassion that led to prayer. God works compassion for others in us when we take our eyes off ourselves. When we see what the Lord sees then compassion will move us as it did Jesus. Compassion is a moving force that leads to action; it is not merely a feeling that only leads to supplication, although it may start there. It is a moving force or power that leads us into intercession. *Prayer in action is intercession. Matthew 10:1 KJV "And when he had called unto him his twelve disciples, he gave them power against unclean spirits, to cast them out, and to heal all manner of sickness and all manner of disease."* Before the disciples could even pray the prayer they were just instructed to pray. Jesus was then making them the answer to what he told them to pray. Remember, Spirit led prayer will always bring about solutions. Sometimes the solutions are quick other times they are not. *Between the time a prayer is prayed and the time it is answered is when patience grows.* Don't lose heart, continue to press into Jesus and do what you know to do in the meantime.

Supplication makes a request, while intercession meets the need. They are both necessary. In the Lord's Prayer or the Our Father, Jesus' disciples are taught to make supplication with reverence. In the same prayer, the answer and the affects of their supplication are manifested. This is all accomplished in one prayer, establishing them in the will of God. When we become forgiven, it frees us from the power of what bound us and the temptation that would have caused us to stumble has no place in us any longer because Jesus has now taken residence in us. Jesus said that *"satan had nothing in Him"*, which is why we can overcome temptation because Jesus lives in us and he overcame temptation for us. In any other Kingdom the people die for the King, in the Kingdom of God the King died for the people. The cross frees us from us, by crucifying the flesh. When we are dead to sin through the cross of Jesus, we are then made alive to God. *Romans 6:11-12 KJV "Likewise reckon ye also yourselves to be dead indeed unto sin, but alive unto God through Jesus Christ our Lord. Let not sin therefore reign in your mortal body, that ye should obey it in the lusts thereof."* The cross of Jesus makes us dead to sin because we have been crucified with him. The concept of being dead in sin is found in Luke 15 when the Good Father is talking to his older son. *Luke 15:24 KJV "For this my son was dead, and is alive again; he was lost, and is found. And they began to be merry." Luke 15:32 KJV "It was meet that we should make merry, and be glad: for this thy brother was dead, and is alive again; and was lost, and is found."* We were dead in sin and now because of Jesus we are dead to sin. We are new creations because the creator of all things gave himself for us, that is really good news.

We are commanded by Jesus to pray *"lead me not into temptation"*. Temptation means "proof or experience of evil, or adversity." The only way to overcome temptation or experience of evil is to no longer partake in evil. This is only done through the working of the cross of Christ. Jesus teaches us the prayer that enables us to deny ourselves, to take up our cross daily and follow him. The daily bread is what allows us to die daily to our will and live for his. Jesus' words are Spirit and Life, causing our flesh to come into subjection continually to make us dead to the flesh and alive to God by His Word, which is fresh daily for those who will listen. There is even a table with bread on it prepared for us to eat at, but who will sit at the table will really surprise you. The daily bread is what allows the dying daily. God's word that is life-giving will also cost us our life, whether it is literally, spiritually or both. Bread is given from the table, just ask Lazarus. After His resurrection from the dead he was one who sat at the table with Jesus, (see John 12:2). The cross delivers us from us, and gets us intimately acquainted with Christ. Jesus had a desire for His closest friends to pray with Him in the Garden. God wants friends who stand and hear the voice of the bridegroom, which is what he has always been looking for. *True worshippers are not merely singers they are listeners* who turn into followers when God says "go". Jesus tells his three best friends that *"He's exceedingly sorrowful even unto death",* and they fall asleep. This is similar to much of what we call "the church" in this hour. Remember this, *if the gates of hell are prevailing it's not the church!* Jesus wakes them up to show His kindness, just as he often does to us. The same thing Jesus told them before He was going to go the cross, is the same thing He says to us before His 2nd coming *"Watch and Pray."* I love the expression watch and pray because it puts the emphasis on listening before speaking. If we have been crucified with Christ, we will be ready for His coming. Those who are ready for his coming can discern his appearing because they have learned to watch and pray. If we have truly learned to watch and pray we will listen and obey. If the cross has marked us, then we will overcome the mark of the beast. It is all so simple, we just pray the Lord's prayer with sincerity in a fear and trembling kind of manner, and he will be sure to lead us to our death, deliver us from self, and give us His very life. When the cross has worked deeply in our life we will echo Jesus' prayer from the tree, *"Father forgive them."* It is our brokenness that releases the fragrance of Christ in the earth. The seed that is broken opened is the seed that rises up. This corporately will happen and Jesus will return for a Bride who has made herself ready, by heeding her Bridegroom's words and praying His prayers. *It is easy to be where God is moving; it is more painful to be what God is doing. Anything that doesn't have a cost is worthless, and will be fruitless.* The Lord's Prayer was spoken about to His disciples, prayed in the secret place of the Garden of Gethsemane, and rewarded openly on the cross. Sometimes our reward is actually a sacrifice so others can enter into blessing.

If our prayer is Spiritual others will benefit from our answered prayer, as did the thief who met Jesus that day in paradise. The prayer of Jesus, *"Father forgive them"* was timely also, because if Jesus hadn't have went to the cross that very day, that man would not have received the forgiveness Jesus asked for when he prayed from the cross. That man would have not been in paradise that day as Jesus prophesied. Remember God's timing is perfect because he is wisdom. We will either be selfish or selfless, depending on if we are crucified with Christ or an enemy of the Cross. The Lord's Prayer sets us up to please God and be in proper relationship with Him. It teaches us to rightly relate to God as our Holy Father and it teaches us to forgive, and even pray for others to be forgiven. This prayer is the model to make us just like Christ.

Now we have met Jesus on the cross, with every ounce of us has been drained out, and we lie dead in a tomb relying totally on the Spirit of God to resurrect us. Now then let us see the dark cold tomb, with the body of Christ lying totally lifeless, wrapped in linen that was once white but is completely soaked through with blood. This is the tomb that the wealthy disciple Joseph of Arimathaea prepared for the body of Christ. As many of Jesus' wealthy disciples still do today. I guess Jesus believes in prosperity, but not covetousness. If you are prosperous, you crave the Body of Christ and will prepare a place for his people. Making room for others is what Jesus did and as his disciples we must do as he did.

Chapter 13
Arise and shine

In Scriptures we see very clearly that God speaks to God. *Matthew 3:16-17 KJV "And Jesus, when he was baptized, went up straightway out of the water: and, lo, the heavens were opened unto him, and he saw the Spirit of God descending like a dove, and lighting upon him: And lo a voice from heaven, saying, This is my beloved Son, in whom I am well pleased."* At the Jordan River, the Godhead had a family reunion. The precious Holy Spirit baptized Jesus in the Jordan River. It was then where the Father said, *"This is my beloved Son in whom I am well pleased."* The Father is pleased when the Holy Spirit comes upon us because he knows the end results of that baptism. In other places in Scripture Jesus prays to the Father, this is again God talking to God. It is very interesting to see how God speaks to God; it is there where we see what perfect unity, respect and honor looks like. Now we go to the tomb where Jesus' body lay; it is cold and really dark in the tomb that Joseph of Arimathaea has prepared for Jesus. We know that Joseph is a wealthy man, but spiritually he was rich also because when Jesus was no longer with him, he still was thinking of Jesus. This disciple's wealth was an instrument of righteousness. Joseph took the body, wrapped it and laid the body in the rock which had been cut out of the stone himself, scripture says that this was Joseph's own new tomb, so Joseph put Jesus where he was going to go. This is the body that Christ would be risen and ascended in, the Father in timeless eternity would forever look at this scarred body that brought many sons to glory. Then Joseph personally rolled a great stone to the door. Joseph, carried Him, wrapped Him, laid Him in the tomb and rolled the stone to the door.

Here, I am sharing a vision I had in the Spirit of my mind. Here lies the body of the Son of God, wrapped in linen soaked in blood, in a cold tomb, lightless and lifeless. Roughly at the end of the Sabbath as it began to dawn, a light that would make the sun look like a light bulb, which moves so fast it creates fire in earth's atmosphere breaks into the visible realm and effortless pierces the tomb, like it was not even there. The person of the Holy Spirit looks at Jesus' body lying their and says, *Arise and shine for your light has come and the Glory of the Lord is risen upon you,* and there Jesus sits up as Holy Spirit, the Spirit of Holiness raises Jesus from the dead.

Remember it is His Light that was the Life of men, and when He was no longer in the earth, neither was His light. I had a vision of this in the Spirit of my mind one day as I was reading the book of Isaiah. I realized it wasn't only meant to encourage some people to rise up, but it literally was God speaking to God. Note, I am not making a doctrine out of this. I was weeping and worshipping God, as the Word of God gripped my heart so hard my eyes began to leak.

After Jesus' resurrection many things occurred, but even the Angel of the Lord had a burden to tell Mary Magdalene and the other Mary that he knew they were seeking the crucified Jesus, who was now risen. Many seek Jesus, but few seek the crucified Jesus. Many seek what Jesus can give to them, but few understand what he did for them and are really willing to fully live for him. Before the Angel of the Lord tells them, "He has risen from the dead," he tells them he knows that they are seeking the crucified Jesus. The Angel of the Lord is obviously aware they are seeking the real Jesus. The Angel of the

Lord who was sent from Heaven, who when he came an Earthquake occurred, even was preaching Christ crucified. This encounter with the Angel of the Lord and Jesus' empty tomb will cause you to run with great fear and joy. When my renewed mind saw that vision, fear and tears of joy overwhelmed me as my heart was gripped by the Spirit that raised Jesus from the dead, opening the scriptures causing my heart to burn within me as Holy Spirit showed me that it is all about Jesus. What is interesting is while they were on their way running with fear and joy; it was while they were running after the Angel's word and the empty tomb that Jesus meets them on the way. These women were known to be at His feet before he was crucified and after He was risen, yet again they found themselves at the same place once again worshiping the one who death could not hold.

Just imagine the passion the Holy Spirit had for Jesus, they had never been separated for all of eternity. Then for three days were separated. The time of their separation must have felt longer than all of eternity past. They were so passionate about one another. Imagine how the Father felt? Jesus never quenched or grieved Holy Spirit; Jesus always did what the Father was doing. I can't even begin to comprehend the Humility of God, how for three days He subject His Eternal passion for His Son and limited Himself and put Himself on a human earthly time schedule for 24 hours a day until the three days were fulfilled, and He sent Holy Spirit to raise Him from the dead. *Isaiah 57:17 KJV "For thus saith the high and lofty One that inhabiteth eternity, whose name is Holy; I dwell in the high and holy place, with him also that is of a contrite and humble spirit, to revive the spirit of the humble, and to revive the heart of the contrite ones."* The God who inhabits all of eternity, subject himself to the futility of time, this is humility beyond understanding. This is the wisdom of God for the redemption of mankind. This is the kind of kindness and goodness that leads men to repentance.

After the resurrection when Mary Magdalene was going to touch Jesus in John 20:17, Jesus says something profound to her. *John 20:17 "Jesus saith unto her, Touch me not; for I am not yet ascended to my Father: but go to my brethren, and say unto them, I ascend to my Father, and your Father; my God, and your God."* I believe this is a picture of the Son's passion for the Father, and the Father's passion for the Son. I can just begin to *imagine* heaven absolutely quiet, with the four living creatures with tears in every one of their eyes, while the Father is embracing His Precious Son, who bears the proof of purchase. The wounds that were given to Him were because God so loved us. I can just see Jesus looking into His Father's eyes saying it was worth it, but it's good to be home. This was probably the most powerful Holy Ghost party yet to date. Jesus may not have wanted Mary to touch him because He wanted to first go back to the bosom of the Father, from where He was sent. Besides Holy Spirit entering into Jesus and raising Him from the dead, I *presume* the Father was the next person to touch Him, in Heaven when they embraced and hugged one another. It went from the Father giving His Son a Cup full of the Wrath of God, to giving Him a hug full of love and possibly accompanied with tears. I can just *imagine* the Father stopping and looking at His Son bearing those wounds remembering the time they were apart, and with Holy and perfect tears on both the Father and Son's face as they embrace. If there is any video recording in Heaven, that's the one my eyes and ears would love to hear and see after I have been given a new body. I don't think our physical body could contain a conversation like that; we may never get up off the floor after that one. Maybe heaven will be like a Charismatic service, where Jesus is the center forever and there's no flaky person looking for attention, who knows? Just a thought.

I love when God undoes people. His kindness just wrecks them and they can barely pick themselves up. God wants to mess us up; he

The Execution of Jesus Christ

did it to Daniel, Isaiah, Ezekiel, and John the Revelator. Those who got "messed up," "undone" or "deeply touched" by God all wound up on their faces. Peter went into a trance that went against everything he was ever taught as a child. The revelation Peter received from this trance, literally became New Testament doctrine, see Acts 10. God wants to mess us up so that we end up looking like Jesus. Isaiah saw the Lord and he was "undone". If God knocked Paul off a horse, God will knock you or I of our horse as well. Briefly we have seen in Scripture of God's passion for himself. God's passion for himself is seen when he talks to himself. Here are some scriptures where God is talking to himself: Genesis 1:26, Genesis 11:1-8, Isaiah 6:8, and Perhaps Isaiah 60:1. In a world that thinks everything is about us, sometimes we bring that mind to the Scripture instead of the mind of Christ. I was just introducing that *perhaps* some Scripture is God talking to God. Maybe Isaiah 60:1 is the Holy Spirit talking to Jesus' dead body and raising him from the dead. I am not making a doctrine out of it so please don't put me on a heresy website. I was just sharing an experience and a thought. I am just bringing up that perhaps there are many Scriptures where God is speaking to God, and perhaps we can see the passion the Godhead has for one another, and possibly learn unity from God who is perfect.

After Jesus was resurrected from the dead he did many things. He appeared to His disciples in another form and they didn't recognize him, see Mark 16:12. The question is can we discern his appearing in our life? He breathed on His disciples before the Holy Spirit blew them away. He opened Scripture to them and caused their hearts to burn. This is very important and is essential before true out pouring. When people in other countries receive dreams and visions, the Lord is simply opening the Scriptures to them without the Bible. By his Holy Spirit he is revealing the truth of his Word in the prophetic realm of dreams and/or visions. Then they tell someone who has a

Bible and they find out where and from whom their dream or vision was from. Often Jesus reveals himself to muslims in a dream or vision. Jesus opened scripture and showed his disciples it was really all about Him, speaking of the Law, the Prophets and the Psalms. I believe the Lord Jesus is doing this right now in the earth like never before. This was truly a privilege, and it was the preparation for them to be forever ruined by what would happen in Acts 2 when suddenly the Holy Spirit came. *When God showed up in the building, the church left the building.* That is another message for another day. Remember when God comes we must be willing to "GO".

Chapter 14

The centrality of true outpouring

The centrality of true Holy Spirit outpouring is Christ Jesus. He is preeminent in all that the Father and his Holy Spirit are doing in the earth. Jesus is the will of the Father. In the center of the Garden of Eden was the Tree of Life. Jesus is this Tree that gives life, he even gave his life on a tree. When John the Revelator sees Jesus, Jesus is in the midst or the center of the throne. When Jesus, the Son of God appears in the fiery furnace in Babylon he appears in the midst of the fire. When Jesus walks through the walls, in John 20:19, when the doors were shut he appeared in the midst of them. Jesus being the center is so vital and important to be able to identify and discern whether what is happening is of God or not. When Jesus was hanging on a cross, he was in the center of the two criminals. It is important to know that Jesus is the center of all God is doing always. When Holy Spirit at the River Jordan baptized Jesus; simultaneously the Father spoke pleasure over the Son. The Father and the Spirit meet at Jesus, the Father says later during another time on the Mount of Transfiguration, *"this is my well beloved Son Hear Him."* The only directive from the Father was "to hear his Son". The Father tells us to hear the Son. While the Holy Spirit brings to our remembrance what Jesus has previously has said. The Father and the Holy Spirit, have a passion that is identical because they are in perfect unity and it is this: that they long for the Son to be honored, and to receive the Glory that he alone is worthy of. In the Godhead there is no insecurity, only perfect unity. That is why Jesus says, *"my Father is even greater than I"*, and *"it is better that I go and send the comforter"*. Jesus gives the highest recommendations to Holy Spirit, even though the Holy Spirit led Jesus into the wilderness to be tempted. Even though Holy Spirit led Jesus directly to a cross, where the Wrath of God would be poured out on him, Jesus was not offended. They were in perfect unity and agreement, the prayer in the garden that Jesus prayed was to illustrate Jesus humanity and his deity at the same time, to show us that our Spirit man is supposed to wholly posses our life in this flesh suite. The moral of the story Jesus is the centrality to any true outpouring. Jesus had a traveling ministry because *he was the move of God.*

Zechariah 12:10 KJV "And I will pour out upon the house of David, and upon the inhabitants of Jerusalem, the Spirit of Grace and supplications: and they shall look upon me whom they have pierced, and they shall mourn for him, as one mourneth for his only son, and shall be in bitterness for him, as one that is in bitterness for his firstborn." We learn that this is Jesus speaking, because scripture teaches us that Jesus was pierced in His hands, feet, and side when nailed to a tree for us, because of God's unfailing love. *God's love is unfailing, which means his word is infallible.* It is just who he is, good. History tells us that this Prophetic encounter that Zechariah the Prophet received when Jesus was telling him some last day outpouring plans He had for the people of Covenant was 487 years before Christ manifested in the flesh, and opened the womb of Mary. The operation of the Holy Spirit causes the people of covenant to look upon the covenant Himself; Holy Spirit puts Jesus on display. The Spirit of Grace and Supplications causes' pleasure and favor to come, stirring earnest and fervent prayer, causing the people of covenant to see Jesus. Prayer is supposed to open our eyes to the beauty of Jesus. Because the Lamb was slain from before the foundation of the world, 487 years before Jesus came out of the womb he said, *"they will look upon me in whom they have pierced"*, past tense. Scripture does not say who they will pierce. In *Zechariah 13:6 KJV "And one shall say unto him, What are these wounds in thine hands? Then he shall answer, Those with which I was wounded in the house of my friends."* The Spirit of Grace and Supplications puts a pierced Jesus on display, bringing mourning. Before Jesus is put on display, grace is released and prayer is made, and a pierced Jesus is the answer. Remember Jesus is the answer and the center. In Zechariah 12:10 Jesus speaks in first person and says *"Me whom they have pierced."* In the gospels Jesus sometimes speaks in third person and refers to himself as *"the Son of Man shall be delivered unto the chief priests."* Holy Spirit will teach you Jesus' language, as he reminds you of His words. Jesus is his absolute favorite topic.

The Spirit of Wisdom and Revelation is the Spirit that unveils or reveals Jesus. Paul prayed this for the Ephesians. Paul's supplication is rooted in Jesus' high priestly prayer. Remember our prayer should be rooted in God's desire, which is why Jesus taught us how to pray. *John 17: 1-3 KJV "These words spoke Jesus, and lifted up his eyes to heaven, and said, Father, the hour is come; glorify thy Son, that thy Son also may glorify thee: As thou hast given him power over all flesh, that he should give eternal life to as many as thou hast given him. And this is life eternal, that they might know thee the only true God, and Jesus Christ, whom thou hast sent."* Jesus is praying to the Father that his disciples would know the Father who Jesus came to reveal. *Ephesians 1:17-18 KJV "That the God of our Lord Jesus Christ, the Father of Glory, may give unto you the spirit of wisdom, and revelation in the knowledge of him: The eyes of your understanding being enlightened; that ye may know what is the hope of his calling, and what the riches of the glory of his inheritance in the saints."* The Him is, Jesus. It is the Father who gives the Holy Spirit to us that we might know and become like Jesus. The very next verse in Ephesians 1:18 talks about the *"eyes of our understanding being enlightened."* The hope of his calling is heard, and the riches of the glory of his inheritance in the saints is seen. Jesus said in *Matthew 13* "*blessed are your ears for they hear and your eyes for they see.*" The question is do we see the treasure in one another? Or do we only see the negative in people? It doesn't take a prophet to tell someone what is wrong with him or her. However it takes faith and enlightened eyes to see riches and treasure God has placed in one another. Jesus didn't see the shell of the pearl; He saw through the shell into the pearl and spent himself on it. Jesus saw beyond the surface, he saw the treasure that was hidden in the field.

God said to Moses in *Numbers 12:6 "And he said, hear now my words: If there be a prophet among you, I will make my self known unto him in a vision, and will speak unto him in a dream."* This again is the operation of the Spirit of wisdom and revelation that makes Jesus known. The ultimate purpose of a Prophet is not Prophecy but a revelation of the Lord Jesus Christ. The book of Joel has a prophecy that is yet to be fully manifested but it is in process. When it is then the end shall come. *Joel 2:28 "And it shall come to pass afterward, that I will pour out my Spirit upon all flesh; and your sons and your daughters shall prophecy, and your old men shall dream dreams, and your young men shall see visions."* God said to Moses "*I will make my self known, through dreams and vision.*" This is happening right now all over the world especially in the Middle East, Jesus is unstoppable. His words are all true, and he is all together lovely. The Spirit of Wisdom and revelation was sent by the Father with the purpose of making his Precious Son known. The main thing about the outpouring of the Spirit and the Prophetic movement must be Christ Jesus. *Those who are fascinated with angels simply do not know Jesus; because the angels are completely fascinated with Jesus, see Isaiah 6.*

The Spirit of Wisdom and Revelation is what was operating upon John the Revelator to make the book of Revelation possible, for it is the revelation of Jesus Christ. John received this in vision form and was commanded to write it down. Remember anointed words are always a picture from God's perspective. The Spirit of Wisdom and Revelation positioned John to receive the book of Revelation, for John was in the Spirit on the Lord's Day. To receive an outpouring is good and it is the beginning of being in the Spirit on the Lord's Day. Ezekiel was in the river and then he was fully submersed in it, see Ezekiel 47. The Spirit of God can be in you or you can be in Him, there is a difference. During Jesus' earthly ministry the Spirit of God was with the disciples. Then Jesus promised the comforter, the Spirit of truth would be in them. In John 20:22 Jesus blew upon his disciples and said to them "receive the Holy Ghost." Then in Acts 2 he blew them away and sent them out. In John 20 they received the indwelling presence of the Holy Spirit, in Acts 2 they received the infilling presence of the Lord. Bill Johnson said this *"The Holy Spirit is in you for you, but he is upon you for them."* What John the revelator would experience in Revelation chapter 1 would be a whole other level of Holy Spirit.

Revelation 1:10 "I was in the Spirit on the Lord's day, and heard behind me a great voice, as of a trumpet." John was where the Lord wanted him, when the Lord wanted him. In the Spirit on the Lord's Day he labored to enter the rest, and on the day of rest he received a Revelation of Jesus in Glory, with eyes like flames of fire. John had experienced the outpouring of the Spirit and the infilling of the Spirit, but now God poured John the beloved into his world. What's interesting is you have a God who was a Jewish man, for Jesus was from the Lineage of Judah. He's the Lion of the tribe of Judah appearing to a Hebrew, on a Hebrew Holy day, the day of rest. While this Hebrew, John, is on a pagan Island for the testimony of Jesus and the Word of God. Jesus describes himself with the pagan alphabet and says, "I am the Alpha and the Omega." Remember Jesus is the savior of all people. His first covenant was with Israel; his last covenant was with all who would believe. Mind you John has never seen Jesus in this form before, on top of that Jesus refers to himself by a name he has used before in a place John has never been before. John can only discern this is Jesus because "his sheep hear his voice and follow." The beloved revelator is old and has gone through the testing of his Faith and has been found faithful. Now he sees his reward, Jesus, and falls at his feet as a dead man. It's interesting how Jesus appears in the middle of the candlestick, which was a familiar object to a Jewish man, describing himself in a pagan language; appearing in a form John has never seen. This must have messed John up. What was John thinking, and what was the purpose of all this? They had already sent him to the Island called Patmos, he had already been thrown in prison and beat, suffered for the gospel, but what was next? Did John have any idea what would come of all this? People now still argue today over John's encounter with the Glorified Jesus. Instead of getting hungry for our own encounter we argue with each other. John most likely had no idea of the ramifications and the privilege he had when he received and wrote the Revelation of Jesus Christ. An elderly man who was deeply persecuted finished what would later be the last book of Bible, wow. God rewarded his faithfulness.

As we look back to the book of Revelation, Jesus is now in the midst of the Candlestick. He is clothed with a garment down to the foot, and girt about his chest with a golden girdle. The Spirit that John was in, on the Lord's timing, is now putting a glorified Jesus on display. Remember the Father and the Holy Spirit love to reveal Jesus; He is their first love. Then the message was for the church in Asia, but it desperately needs to be heard today. Here is what the Holy Spirit presented to John. *Revelation 1:14-17 KJV "His head and his hairs were white like wool, as white as snow; and his eyes were as flames of fire; And his feet like unto fine brass, as if they burned in a furnace; and his voice as the sound of many waters. And he had in his right hand seven stars: out of his mouth went a sharp two-edged sword: and his countenance was as the sun shineth in his strength."* This is the glorified Jesus, which John fell at his feet as a dead man. The point is now the Holy Spirit is putting a glorified Jesus on display, with a message as sharp like the two-edged sword in his mouth. The double-edged sword in his mouth is a picture of the Spirit of Truth. The question is will the church receive the outpouring of these words or chose the outpouring of strong delusion? (See 2 Thessalonians 2:7-11) This outpouring of the Spirit leads to a sobering message. The outpouring of the Spirit and the words of Jesus are eternally inseparable. *Proverbs 1:23 KJV "Turn you at my reproof: behold, I will pour out my spirit unto you, I will make known my words unto you."* Here is another example of this truth. *John 6:63 KJV "It is the spirit that quickeneth; the flesh profiteth nothing: the words that I speak unto you, they are spirit, and they are life."*

Revelation chapters 2 and 3 were to realign the church with the Kingdom. Today this is greatly needed like never before. *Receiving correction is what protects us from deception.* Not receiving the truth is what causes God himself to send strong delusion. *2 Thessalonians 2:10-12 KJV "And with all deceivableness of unrighteousness in them that perish; because they received not the love of the truth, that they might be saved. And for this cause God shall send them strong delusion, that they should believe a lie: That they all might be damned who believed not the truth, but had pleasure in unrighteousness."* Remember this is taking place while God is also pouring out his Spirit on all flesh because he doesn't desire that any should perish. *I Samuel 16:13-14 KJV "Then Samuel took the horn of oil, and anointed him in the midst of his brethren: and the Spirit of the LORD came upon*

David from that day forward. So Samuel rose up, and went to Ramah. But the Spirit of the LORD departed from Saul, and an evil spirit from the LORD troubled him." God poured out his Spirit upon David and sent an evil tormenting Spirit to Saul. 2 Thessalonians 2:10-12 is a New Testament parallel of the same truth. This is similar to God's judgment upon Egypt and his mercy for Israel. Remember wheat and tears are in the same filed until the appointed time.

When John was poured into the Spirit He saw a glorified Jesus. It takes humility to go this deep in God. We must position ourselves directly in the right time, in the right place to receive like this from the Lord. To simplify all the positioning talk. We must have a listening ear and a heart that is willing and obedient. If we learn how to listen we will be in the right position. Everything must be surrendered to God for this to occur. Cost determines value; John had to go through a lot to even be able to bear this message in his Spirit. Previously John was rebuking a man during Jesus' earthly ministry because he wasn't traveling with Jesus. *Luke 9:49-50 KJV "And John answered and said, Master, we saw one casting out devils in thy name; and we forbad him, because he followeth not with us. And Jesus said unto him, Forbid him not: for he that is not against us is for us."* John knew he was going to bear a strong rebuke, but his very life had to become the wineskin that could contain and release this in God's timing. This is a good picture of an unsanctified calling. There are some in the body of Christ that are just like John trying to tell people to stop what they are doing because they couldn't do it or failed trying to do it, see the story before Luke 9:37-43. *The church of Jesus today needs to hear that message,* "he that is not against us is for us." Often when we leave our first love and the front lines we become really good at shooting our brother in the foot and seeing the speck in our brothers eye. I know this from being guilty of it myself. How about you? If so, repent and refocus your attention on Jesus.

The Spirit of Prophecy in Revelation 19:10 opens heaven, and then presents the picture of Christ's supremacy. The context is very important to see if we are going to learn a great lesson from these scriptures. *Revelation 19:9-11 KJV "And he said unto me. Write Blessed are they which are called unto the marriage supper of the Lamb. And he said unto me, these are the true sayings of God. And I fell at his feet to worship him. And he said unto me, see thou do it not: I am thy fellow servant, and of thy brethren that have the testimony of Jesus: worship God: for the testimony of Jesus is the Spirit of Prophecy. And I saw heaven opened, and behold a white horse; and he that sat upon him was called Faithful and True, and in righteousness he doth make war."* Some real powerful revelation comes to John and he's about to bow down to a saint and the saint says don't do it, and declares the Testimony of Jesus is the Spirit of Prophecy. Immediately heaven opens and John sees Jesus on a white horse, with eyes like flames of fire, and now he's crowned with many crowns about to make war on the earth. The Spirit of Prophecy puts a Jesus on display that sits on a white horse, who is crowned with many crowns. *Jesus is crowned with many crowns because he is the King of Kings. All authority belongs to him because he is the King of Kings and the Lord of lords. When he surrendered all of his will the Father gave him all of his authority.* Man is prone to worship man, so John is about to bow to this dude who is not an Angel, because angels are not created in the image of God, as brethren are. This saint says don't do it. So if anyone did have an encounter with heaven or a saint, that saint would not allow us to pray to him or her, but rather tell us to worship God, and to keep us from error. Then the Holy Spirit would present Jesus to us in a fresh way, which would quickly show us that Jesus alone is worthy. The Spirit of Prophecy is to reveal Christ's supremacy. He humbled himself unto the death of the cross and now is subduing all things under his feet through his highly exalted name. That is good news and it's for you and your family.

Chapter 15
Living in the reward of His suffering

Christ suffered for us and we will also sufferer for him, for if we suffer with him we shall reign with him. True training for reigning is suffering. *1 Peter 4:1-2 KJV "Forasmuch then as Christ hath suffered for us in the flesh, arm yourselves likewise with the same mind: for he that hath suffered in the flesh hath ceased from sin; That he no longer should live the rest of his time in the flesh to the lusts of men, but to the will of God."* As the end of the age swiftly approaches there will be a wave of Martyrdom. Several things bring about the end of the age, the day and the hour no man knows. The Gospel of the Kingdom will be preached in the entire world and then the end shall come, see Matthew 24:14. We must not worry about the end, but we should hasten the day by the preaching of the gospel and a holy life of true intercession. Before the end of the age prophecy must be fulfilled and the bride must make herself ready, see Revelation 19:7. In case you haven't noticed the bride is certainly not ready, especially when most believers are afraid to evangelize or say, "that's not my calling". As the bride becomes ready she will no longer be afraid of death, or dying for the one she sings and prays to. When we are really a living sacrifice, we are not afraid to die. *Revelation 6:9-11 KJV "And when he had opened the fifth seal, I saw under the altar the souls of them that were slain for the word of God, and for the testimony which they held: And they cried with a loud voice, saying,*

How long, O Lord, holy and true, dost thou not judge and avenge our blood on them that dwell on the earth? And white robes were given unto every one of them; and it was said unto them, that they should rest yet for a little season, until their fellow servants also and their brethren, that should be killed as they were, should be fulfilled." Over the last 200 years martyrdom for the sake of Jesus and the gospel of his Kingdom has greatly increased to the highest amounts of people ever. In spite of great suffering and persecution the glory of the latter house will be greater than that of the former. Of the increase of his Government and peace there shall be no end. A very probable reason the two prophets of Revelation 11 will be killed is because their power is superior to the lying sign and wonders the man of perdition will do, see 2 Thessalonians 2:7-11 and Revelation 11:3-13.

In the midst of the nations being in derision *God sits in the heavens and laughs,* and if we're in him we might also. We have lived with so much less than what Jesus suffered so much to give us. As a church, we are called to live in the reward of Christ's suffering, which is the outpouring of the Holy Spirit. Constantly being filled with the Holy Spirit. If we are not overflowing on the world around us perhaps we are not as filled with the Spirit as we think. Dreams and visions scripture being opened to us by the resurrected Jesus, Healing and miracles should all be normal. That is the only kind of Christianity found in the New Testament. The standard has been lowered which is truly dishonoring to Jesus and his precious Holy Spirit. *Compromise is the behavior of cowards;* we must repent and welcome the Holy Spirit to bring back the standard. *Isaiah 59: 19 KJV "So shall they fear the name of the LORD from the west, and his glory from the rising of the sun. When the enemy shall come in like a flood, the Spirit of the LORD shall lift up a standard against him."* This prophecy is for now. The fear of the Lord is almost completely gone from the Western Church. The Holy Spirit will bring back the revelation of Jesus Christ to the forefront of all we do if our lives are going to have the Father's signature on it. Jesus is the standard and our lives must reflect him if we call Jesus Christ our Lord. Walking in truth is not merely saying Jesus is Lord, but his Lordship must be visible and manifest in our lives.

True prosperity is to be filled with the Spirit enough to overflow Jesus on the world around us. John the Revelator after He saw Jesus, in almost every way possible, said that *"I wish above all things that thou mayest prosper and be in health, even as thy soul prospereth."* Prosperity is law in the kingdom of God; even though the Kingdom belongs to the poor economically and the poor in Spirit spiritually. Wherever Jesus is there is always enough. (For those of you who have not read Heidi Baker's book, "There is always enough" you definitely should.) Jesus starts off with five loaves and two fish and over 5,000 people and ends up with 12 baskets too much. Remember of the increase of his government and peace there shall be no end! God takes Israel out of Egypt, they have enough Gold to build the temple and Moses says, keep the change we don't need anymore for the temple. God sends manna to Israel, and they can't even eat it all. The Abundant life Jesus talks about is the Knowledge of God, because Jesus describes "life" as "knowing God, and Jesus Christ whom thou have sent." We are supposed to be filled with the knowledge of God to the point it leaks out of us and covers the earth we live on. There is spiritual blessings, and gifts that Jesus paid a dear price to give us, we should receive them with thanksgiving and steward them with wisdom. Jesus never called in sick; I personally don't believe we ever have to be sick period. In the book of Acts Peter wasn't sick, but his shadow healed the sick. Some people would say what about Job, and I would say, Job is not my Savior Jesus is. What about Jesus and his stripes, besides what Job feared came upon him. Jesus feared God, and the Spirit of God stayed upon him. What we fear will come upon us, so if we return to the fear of the Lord we can rest assured a historic Holy Spirit outpouring will surely come upon this generation.

The reality is that man makes excuses to excuse their unbelief when they reap the fruit of what they really believe. *Unbelief is one of the biggest devils that invade the church. When the church is not invading it gets invaded.* There are doctrines, which create a culture of unbelief and make up whole denominations to cater to unbelief. Jesus gave his life so we can partake of his divine nature; this is speaking of Character if you read the scriptures in context. However God's character and his power are inseparable. We need character and power. *Without character we have no credibility, without power our message has no validity.* Jesus' first assignment to Adam in the Garden of Eden was creative in nature, and God left Adam some room to name the animals what he wanted to. God didn't give him a photocopied list and a choir. He gave him an assignment that was creative in nature. When the Blood of the Lamb redeems the human soul, the freedom and creativity that the Spirit of the Lord brings by the spoken word of God becomes more influential inside the heart and mind of the believer. Witty inventions were supposed to be for people of covenant, not unredeemed men who believe the ideas God gives more than believers. *The church of Jesus Christ is supposed to manifest God's Kingdom and dominion in every form of society, until they either want Jesus or want to kill us.* We are supposed to be at the cutting edge of every form of society. Such as architecture, music, energy, entertainment, and technology. We are supposed to show the world holy fashion where people are covered, not half naked. The counselor who lives in us supposes us to council the world. Christians are not supposed to go to the word for counsel. Friends, we must awake to righteousness. If the cross hasn't redeemed every area of our life we are living with a lot less than Jesus suffered for. What Jesus did and the ramifications are so unspoken of in the church today it is sick, which perhaps is why a lot of the church is physically sick. *1 Corinthians 11:26 KJV "For as often as ye eat this bread, and drink this cup, ye do show the Lord's death till he come."* The message of the cross must be preached and demonstrated. In Matthew 5-7 Jesus taught his disciples to live the crucified life by loving your enemies and blessing those who curse you.

Acts 2 was the beginning of the reward of Jesus' suffering for the church. The disciples were given miracle power before the cross. However when it was time to stand by Jesus at the cross they all left, but one. The power given in Acts 2 was power to become a "witness or a martyr". Jesus blew on them when he was resurrected and *"said receive ye the Holy Ghost."* This was a deposit of his very life. This was the indwelling presence of the Lord. Then he told them to *"wait in Jerusalem until you are clothed with power from on high."* So they did, and suddenly a wind came and blew them away and they no longer loved their lives. They no longer had any fear of persecution, and many of them wound up on a cross themselves and others were martyred. The fruit of Jesus' laid down life for his friends wasn't just salvation, but also friends who lay down their lives for the one who gave his life for them. This wind that came blew them away so only Christ remained. They were literally blown away. We will either get blown away or carried away, like John the Revelator and Ezekiel, or we will fall away. I believe God will finish the work he began in us. In the days of the tower of Babel, which literally means confusion, we see men trying to get to God their way. God sent confusion and broke their communication and scattered them abroad. Now in this upper room you have a 120 men from every nation represented, and God comes to them and restores the communication. Tongues of fire rested on them, I believe this was fire from the altar that God sent to cleanse their mouths, see Isaiah 6:6-8. The Angel took a coal from the Altar and cleansed Isaiah's mouth. Now I believe the Lord was sending fire from that same Altar and corporately cleansing their mouths and sanctifying their mouths to preach his word. God restored communication, breaking confusion or the curse of Babel, and brought true unity through his Holy Spirit. Uniting people his way, for his purpose, in his timing according to what he had said through the mouth of Joel his prophet.

The author of confusion is satan. The power of satan was broken when God restored communication back to the people created in his image. One of the most amazing things about being created in the image and likeness of God is the ability to communicate with him. All of the people were speaking and proclaiming the mighty acts of God. Praise is the universal language of heaven. The enemy used to be the leader of praise but not any more. Through the death and resurrection of Christ and the power of the Holy Spirit the sting of death was gone. The same men who ran under the threat of persecution now were going to be able to be strong in the Lord and in the power of his might. Those in the upper room were totally ruined by God so much so that men think they were drunk on wine. They weren't drunk on wine, but they were intoxicated with the goodness of God. They truly came under the full influence of the Holy Spirit. Their old life was blown away and their human thought was drowned by the river of God. The fire of God forever marked them as the Holy Spirit came and rested on them.

Jesus was pierced so we can come into him. He offered His Spirit on the cross, and so after we die on our cross we can receive his Spirit. Not only should we live life in the benefits of his suffering, but must also bring him the reward of his suffering. The reward of his sufferings is people created in his image and likeness. The full reward of Jesus' suffering will be in heaven at the Marriage supper, but here on earth it looks like this. *Revelation 12:11 KJV "And they overcame him by the blood of the Lamb, and the word of their testimony, and they loved not their lives unto the death."* The reward of Christ's suffering is that we become willing to suffer and willing to give our life for Jesus and those who he tasted death for. When we love not our life is when we can be faithful stewards of the Mysteries of God. As ministers of Christ we have been given a ministry of reconciliation. There is room in the Father's house, Jesus has paid the price for them and he has also prepared a place for them. He gave us his Holy Spirit and said, "go" and invite them that my house may be full, and so we must "go" if we are going to bring him the reward of his suffering. We, the joy set before him, are commissioned to bring him those he suffered for. You are called, chosen and ordained. The world is waiting for you, so go in Jesus name and get them that the Father's house may be full.

Chapter 16

The soon coming tension and the righteous judgments of God

The tension that was on Jesus' physical body when he was on the cross will soon come to the face of the whole earth. The fullness of the wrath of God that was in the cup that Jesus drank is now in seven golden vials in the temple of the tabernacle of the testimony in Heaven. *Revelation 15:7-8 KJV "And one of the four beasts gave unto the seven angels seven golden vials full of the wrath of God, who liveth for ever and ever. And the temple was filled with smoke from the glory of God, and from his power; and no man was able to enter into the temple, till the seven plagues of the seven angels were fulfilled."* As the scriptures say one of the four living creatures will hand seven gold vials full of the wrath of God, to seven angels that will pour it out on the earth when the time is right according to the will of God. Before this, many interesting events will take place. One specifically fascinates my heart and really makes me see the greatness of the Lord Jesus Christ. This causes me to approach God in a thankful manner with fear and trembling.

Scripture tells us that creation groans according to Romans 8:22. *All of creation is groaning for us to become like the Christ who lives in us.* Groaning is a manifestation of the Holy Spirit in a believer during prayer, see Romans 8:26. Earlier we learned that the disciple's prayers lead to preaching. We also learned that Jesus' "thy will be done" prayer led him to a cross and one of the men next to him to paradise. Prayer leads to salvation, but someone or something's got to preach. Let's look at one more Holy Spirit out pouring and see who the preacher is.

> *Joel 2:28-32 KJV "And it shall come to pass afterward, that I will pour out my Spirit upon all flesh; and your sons and your daughters shall prophecy, your old men shall dream dreams, your young men shall see visions: And also upon the servants and upon the handmaids in those days will I pour out my Spirit. And I will show wonders in the heavens and in the earth, blood and fire, and pillars of smoke. The sun shall be turned into darkness, and the moon into blood, before the great and terrible day of the Lord come. And it shall come to pass, that whosoever shall call on the name of the Lord shall be delivered: for in Mount Zion and in Jerusalem shall be deliverance, as the Lord hath said, and in the remnant who the Lord shall call."*

Here there is an outpouring of the Spirit, which leads to dreams and visions. Then later people are calling upon the name of the Lord. In this there is a message and it is the Lord is Lord of heaven and earth. The earth is the Lord's and the fullness thereof. I call this sermon the "Earth's altar call". *If someone or something intercedes, it should preach as well or it is defective.*

When Jesus was on the cross, the sun no longer gave its light. This is similar to what will happen in this prophecy God spoke through the mouth of his prophet Joel. However when Jesus was on the cross, there was no mention of the moon's activity. The moon turns to blood in Joel's prophecy. Referring to the scripture above, in the book of Joel the Hebrew word there for "blood" that is used is actually "innocent blood", the only blood that is innocent blood is the blood of the Lamb. The earth itself will show all the inhabitants of the earth the Blood of Jesus. The innocent blood will be seen in the heavens and God will use the moon, which is the lesser light according to the book of Genesis. You think because Jesus is the Light of the World maybe he would have used the Sun to preach the Son. Absolutely not, God uses the foolish things. Look, you are reading a book that I wrote; I told you God uses the foolish things. In this prophetic scripture the moon turns to blood and people begin calling on the name of the Lord and being delivered or saved. I hope to be here to see this sermon. The rocks will cry out if we don't. Not only does creation groan it preaches also. The earth was created by God therefore it will be used by him as well in his redemptive purposes and in his judgments. Even the creation testifies of the sacrifice of the creator himself. God using the earth for his purposes, which is in a few other places in the Bible, is an interesting topic. Like when the earth opened up and swallowed Korah's rebellion, for rising up against Moses and offering strange fire.

The heavens declare the Glory of God, and the moon puts the innocent Blood of the Lamb on display causing salvation to those who call upon the name of the Lord Jesus Christ. What a sermon that will be, it is the speechless sermon; it doesn't say the moon will talk but the Blood of Jesus speaks, he who has ears to hear let them hear. Remember you were bought with the very Blood of Christ. He bought us to spend us. He bought us to redeem us and make us part of his redemptive plan. We have all fallen short of his glory, but the Blood of Jesus brings us near. The Blood speaks, "You will not love your life, you will not love your life even unto death." Remember a Lamb lives in you, and his longing is to lay down his life so you can walk worthy of the calling. Christ in you is the Hope of glory. You may be the only hope your neighbor has to escape hell's fire and enter into the eternal Kingdom of God our Father through his only begotten and well beloved Son Jesus. I encourage you to open your mouth and let Jesus come forth. If you open your mouth he will fill it, that his Father's house may be full. Remember you can do all things through Christ who strengthens you and you are his beloved.

Chapter 17
They that are Christ's

"Christ crucified is the rarest piece of knowledge in the world." Isaac Ambrose 1551 A.D

Galatians 5:24 KJV *"And they that are Christ's have crucified the flesh with the affections and lusts."* The Apostle Paul is laying out a clear way to discern those who are fully possessed by Christ Jesus. Jesus purchased us to possess us wholly, not to borrow us for religious activity on Sunday morning. The crucified life is the only life where resurrection power is attainable and sustainable. I will roughly quote Watchman Nee; he said *"the blood of Jesus is for your sin, while the cross is for your flesh."* To fully love God with all our strength, our flesh must be crucified. Like Jacob, God wants us to walk with a limp. Jacob's encounter with the Angel of the Lord is a good picture of having a crucified flesh. It's hard to put confidence in the flesh when you walk with a limp. Many people in church have no idea that wrestling with God in prayer will cause you to walk with a limp. When a person's flesh is crucified their main desire is to communicate with God. This person understands where his life, strength and help comes from. Most of what happens today in church is flesh with a touch of Jesus. How much of our services can be done without Jesus? You can get a Greek/Hebrew study Bible and get a nice little message. You can have a trained musician play two fast songs and two slow songs and out you go. Where was Jesus in all that? The same place he was in Laodicea, knocking on the door of his church. *Jesus wants his church back.*

Adam LiVecchi

When our flesh is crucified we care less about pleasing people and more about pleasing God. We become less concerned with programs and more concerned with God's presence. Fasting is a part of the crucified life. One of the ways we love God with all of our strength is by empting our strength by fasting. As hunger for Jesus grows you will go on an extended water fast. What you will experience during the fast is the taste of flesh in your mouth. When you have not eaten for quite some time, you will begin to taste your own flesh, it is then you will begin to understand why we are to put no confidence in the flesh. For all my charismatic, conference-going shofar blowing friends, here is a brief illustration concerning the flesh. I bought a shofar and blew it to be really spiritual; there was just something about it that deeply intrigued me. So one day I put my nose in it and it smelled like a dead person with sweaty feet. If there is no laughter in your church it's ok, you can laugh while you read this book. This was dead animal flesh in the ram's horn that I smelled. It smelled horrible and the Lord whispered to me "that is what un-crucified flesh smells like to me." So to try to get rid of the smell I would pour anointing oil in it to try to cover the smell and it never worked. Here is a lesson I learned from this failure to subdue the stench of the flesh. The anointing doesn't flow properly unless the flesh is crucified. To get rid of the dead old flesh in the ram's horn I used bleach and it worked just fine. After the flesh was gone, the ram's horn could smell like the sweet costly anointing oil that was being poured in. We cannot be lead by the Spirit if we don't first crucify the flesh. To be resurrected we must first be dead. Jesus was anointed for burial, when we are anointed it is to bring about a death in us so Christ can live his life through us.

For Christ Jesus to live through us, the lusts and affections must also be crucified. The affections aren't necessarily bad, however lust is. Affections can be bad if they are not crucified, but they are not inherently bad like lusts are. Affections would be how you love your mom or little sister, while a lust would be an evil desire you have for a woman who is at church who isn't dressed in a very Christian like manner. When you see "sister let it all hang out" you may have a pull on your heart and a focusing of your eyes where they need not be, this is lust. To follow Christ you must love him more than your father, mother and friends. You must love him more than your opinions or the opinions of others. If we are going to follow Jesus, we obviously must love him enough to keep our eyes off of "sister let it all hangout." Or for the ladies brother "his shirt is to tight." It's necessary to leave our sinful lifestyle behind as well as our love for family, friends and anything that keeps us from full obedience to Christ. The rich young ruler could not follow Jesus because he had too much stuff. His lusts kept him from following Jesus. He could go back to church or the synagogue and no one would have known that he passed the opportunity of a lifetime up, but Jesus would always know the truth. We can totally deny Jesus personally and fit in with a group of religious people with no problem. Many people have done it in church for twenty years, denying what God has put in their heart. One of the benefits of having crucified affections is that you cannot be offended. When someone is offended it is telling us that their affections are not crucified because they still feel they have the right to be offended. Our affections can get infected if they are not crucified. Paul the Apostle said, *"I am crucified with Christ."* The cross of Christ didn't just crucify Jesus, but it crucified you and I if we are truly his. The world is also crucified to us because we are His possession. As His possession we must present our bodies as a living sacrifice, because he did. After Jesus' resurrection he still bore in his body the proof of his crucifixion, which is the proof of our purchase as I have mentioned previously. Crucifixion is to bring forth resurrection. Jesus said, *"I am the resurrection and the life."*

What's funny is Jesus said that before he died and rose again. He has the best personality ever; if you don't believe me just ask Our Father or the Holy Spirit. We are to pass from death to life, so Christ is glorified through us. If we are in him then he will certainly move through us, and that is what the world needs.

Chapter 18
None should perish

We, as believers, need to unite our will with God's, which is true Christianity. The world around us won't know it is true until we start living it out and demonstrating Jesus to the poor, the sick and the perishing. Charles Spurgeon, who was nicknamed "the prince of preachers", said this," *If sinners be damned, at least let them leap to Hell over our dead bodies. And if they perish, let them perish with our arms wrapped about their knees, imploring them to stay. If Hell must be filled, let it be filled in the teeth of our exertions, and let not one go unwarned and unprayed for."* That is love speaking. We need to hear a whole lot more of this kind of preaching today and less of the itchy ear, man-pleasing, sissified-seeker-sensitive nonsense. In many churches the devil himself can come in and sit down and feel right at home, he did it in the book of Revelation. What I love about Haiti is that the devil can't hide there. As praise and worship goes on the demonized begin to manifest and become exposed in the presence of God and his Kingdom. Religion can suppress the demonic, the devil can even sit right next to the religious, but when Jesus comes to town all the monkeys in the closet must come out. Hear the greatest lover ever speak to his church that he so desperately wanted back.

Revelation 2:13-16 KJV "I know thy works, and where thou dwellest, even where Satan's seat is: and thou holdest fast my name, and hast not denied my faith, even in those days wherein Antipas was my faithful martyr, who was slain among you, where Satan dwelleth. But I have a few things against thee, because thou hast there them that hold the doctrine of Balaam, who taught Balac to cast a stumblingblock before the children of Israel, to eat things sacrificed unto idols, and to commit fornication. So hast thou also them that hold the doctrine of the Nicolaitans, which thing I hate. Repent; or else I will come unto thee quickly, and will fight against them with the sword of my mouth."

False doctrine is the seat of satan. He is the Father of lies, and wherever lies are he is also. I wonder if satan was sitting in the back of this church, or in the front row next to the Pastor and his wife? Was he sitting in the youth group? Did he prefer to sit with the elders and the big financial givers who try to control the Pastor in the name of Jesus for accountability's sake? Jesus himself will fight against the church that fails to repent and tolerates sin and false doctrine. I don't hear much talk about this kind of Jesus in church today, do you?

Unfortunately in these days the preaching of the true gospel needs to be preached in the church as bad as it needs to be preached in the world. The good news is the church is getting hungry for Jesus and his kingdom that is here and coming. Many people in the church today are like the men that came to David when he was in the cave of Adullam.

1 Samuel 22: 1-2 KJV "David therefore departed thence, and escaped to the cave Adullam: and when his brethren and all his father's house heard it, they went down thither to him. And every one that was in distress, and every one that was in debt, and every one that was discontented, gathered themselves unto him; and he became a captain over them: and there were with him about four hundred men."

They are sick of religious games, control, manipulation and every other kind of evil that is manifested when people don't obey Jesus and don't seek to advance his Kingdom at all costs. David was among the priests but there was a spy from Saul who spotted him and he had to flee from religion. When true leadership runs from religion, the hungry and the disenfranchised gather. I believe this is happening in the body of Christ in these days.

The world is perishing and much of the church is starving. The stage is set for true Spiritual hunger to fully overtake a generation of people. This generation has no age limitations, the only thing that really matters is their spiritual hunger for Jesus and their willingness to obey and partner with his ever increasing the Kingdom. God is raising up preachers of righteousness who will be full of love, but also as bold as a lion. They will speak the truth in love like Stephen the martyr. He called the Jews names but was willing to forgive them and bleed for them even as they stoned him, see Acts 7:1-60.

Most of the American church has an unbiblical concept of love, which is called deception. Anytime you confront someone about his or her behavior all of a sudden you are not loving. Those are the very same people that will talk behind your back all night at a prayer meeting in the name of Jesus, because they are concerned about you. In church they will smile at you and say I love you "brother", but do they really? The sissified preaching is a sign to the lost that we don't really love as much as we think we do. Here is another quote on the same topic from the Prince of Preachers *"Let eloquence be flung to the dogs rather than souls be lost. What we want is to win souls. They are not won by flowery speeches."* The preaching of the Gospel and the demonstration of the Spirit with power are God's prescription for both the lost and the church. Keep in mind the next scripture you are going to read is Jesus speaking to the church in the city of Ephesus roughly 96 years after his resurrection. The church in those days was more regional than denominational, God have mercy on us. God doesn't see denominational lines he sees division and deception. Many would say, "we don't split over doctrine", but Jesus said *"I will fight against you with the sword of my mouth, unless you repent."* It has been said that, *"it is the unity of the Spirit and not the unity of doctrine."* Ok my question is, if it's the Spirit of truth that unifies us and lives in us perhaps someone is wrong? The true church are those who the gates of hell are not prevailing against, he knows his own and they know, act, and smell like him. They are those who live with his character and move in his power. When we are really focused on Jesus love, power and sound doctrine come naturally by the Spirit of truth Jesus provided for us.

A truly regional church can only be regional by their commitment to the preaching of the gospel and the advancement of God's Kingdom here on earth, at all costs. Anything else is denominational and values thoughts more than action, and gathering together more than obeying Jesus together.

> *Revelation 2:2-5 KJV "I know thy works, and thy labor, and thy patience, and how thou canst not bear them which are evil: and thou hast tried them which say they are apostles, and are not, and hast found them liars: And hast borne, and hast patience, and for my name's sake hast labored, and hast not fainted. Nevertheless I have somewhat against thee, because thou hast left thy first love. Remember therefore from whence thou art fallen, and repent, and do the first works; or else I will come unto thee quickly, and will remove thy candlestick out of his place, except thou repent."*

Ephesus is modern day Turkey, which is about 98 % muslim today. Perhaps the lamp stand was removed? Here Jesus is realigning the church with his Kingdom through his word. The word of the King aligns the church with the Kingdom, if we would only change the way they think. I call this church *"discernment international, church of the log in our eye".* They could discern false apostles but couldn't discern they had lost their first love and left their first work. When we truly have oil in our lamp there will be light in the world. When there is no oil in our lamp, there is no light in the world and unless we repent the lamp stand will be removed. They could see the error of false apostles but were unfamiliar with the affections of their own heart toward the one who gave himself for them. We are never like them, or are we? The connection between loss of first love, focusing on false apostles and leaving their first work is profound and very visible in the church today. When a church doesn't care for the lost and the poor, it is sick and needs to be healed. It is nothing to feel shameful about for Jesus has stripes so we can be healed. Our part is to confess. Jesus will help us to change they way we think if we are willingly to live according to his word by his Holy Spirit that leads us into all truth and comforts us on the journey.

The first love, first works connection is very inseparable biblically speaking. The poor, sick and perishing of our community can tell you how much we really love Jesus. Love is more of an action and a lifestyle than a word or a feeling. Love speaks and is a tangible feeling but love acts on behalf of others. True love is God's pursuit of the disenfranchised, the sick, the poor and the lost, just ask Jesus. Jesus is the love of God manifested. First Jesus had to say, *"it is finished"* before Paul could write, *"love never fails."* If *love never fails* that means it is doing something that it has the possibility to fail at, but does not. Love never fails because Jesus has risen from the dead.

1 Thessalonians 1:2-5 KJV "We give thanks to God always for you all, making mention of you in our prayers; Remembering without ceasing your work of faith, and labor of love, and patience of hope in our Lord Jesus Christ, in the sight of God and our Father; Knowing, brethren beloved, your election of God. For our gospel came not unto you in word only, but also in power, and in the Holy Ghost, and in much assurance; as ye know what manner of men we were among you for your sake."

When the word becomes flesh in us, our life becomes the message of Christ Jesus to the perishing. When the message and the vessel are one, you then have an authentic mature Christian. That is what creation is groaning for. Through us they see him, which is what God is looking for. That is a true worshipper. There are many Christian musicians but very few worshippers.

2 Peter 3:9 KJV "The Lord is not slack concerning his promise, as some men count slackness; but is longsuffering to us-ward, not willing that any should perish, but that all should come to repentance." Recently Jesus spoke to me and said, *"Adam, I am not willing that any should perish but you still are."* This wounded me and brought me to tears, but also gave me hope because he said "you still are," which means if I continue to walk with Jesus one day I will really become like him. Jesus was telling me, "I haven't learned to love like him yet." This caused me to pray, "Lord Jesus, teach me to love like you do and be willing to fully give myself that others may know who you really are." Jesus came to seek and to save that which is lost, he came for the sick. When we are sick all we can think of is ourselves, and what happens inside the four walls of what we call church. There is a shift coming to the church and it is upon us now. For we have sowed much and have reaped little, it is time to reconsider our ways. Not to worry, God's grace is towards us to empower us to become like Jesus and change. One of the primary changes is the church will return to Jesus and the advancement of his Kingdom through the proclamation, demonstration and explanation of the gospel.

Jesus is so willing that none should perish he tasted death for every man. *Hebrews 2:8-10 KJV "Thou hast put all things in subjection under his feet. For in that he put all in subjection under him, he left nothing that is not put under him. But now we see not yet all things put under him. But we see Jesus, who was made a little lower than the angels for the suffering of death, crowned with glory and honor; that he by the grace of God should taste death for every man."* This verse reveals God's heart in that none have to perish because Jesus tasted death for every man. What Jesus accomplished through tasting death was enough. We need to focus on Jesus, instead of focusing on what is not appearing to be under his authority or influence. Our assignment is to bring everything under his authority and influence by the preaching of the Gospel. *Mark 16:15 KJV "And he said unto them, Go ye into all the world, and preach the gospel to every creature."* We are commanded, not suggested, to preach to every creature. Jesus commanded this because the Father loved them and he himself tasted death for them, that they through our obedience and the movement of the Holy Spirit might taste and see that he is good. *Matthew 28:18-20 KJV "And Jesus came and spoke unto them, saying, All power is given unto me in heaven and in earth. Go ye therefore, and teach all nations, baptizing them in the name of the Father, and of the Son, and of the Holy Ghost: Teaching them to observe all things whatsoever I have commanded you: and, lo, I am with you always, even unto the end of the world. Amen."* We are to preach the Kingdom and teach all people to observe and obey all things the King has said. This is our mission, should we choose to be real Christians and obey God.

Jesus believed in you enough to die for you. Therefore I agree with him and believe in you as well. The sacrifice of Jesus on the cross is what opens up the privilege of his Kingdom to all people who will believe on him. The grandeur of his Kingdom is merely an overflow of how good he really is. Jesus wasn't just pored out unto death, but he is overflowing life everlasting. Jesus is the bread of life. When he feed the multitude with five loaves and two fish it was the Father prophetically saying, "lunch is on me, there is enough of Jesus for all who would come and eat and drink." *Revelation 22:1-2 KJV "And he showed me a pure river of water of life, clear as crystal, proceeding out of the throne of God and of the Lamb. In the midst of the street of it, and on either side of the river, was there the tree of life, which bare twelve manner of fruits, and yielded her fruit every month: and the leaves of the tree were for the healing of the nations."* The healing of the nations can only come thought the personal salvation of people created in his image. Healing comes to us when we become subject to Jesus. You are a part of God's plan of bringing healing to the nations, so go and preach and demonstrate Jesus. You are set apart, this is your calling; you are chosen so be faithful.

> *"God has set apart His people from before the foundation of the world to be His chosen and peculiar inheritance. We are sanctified in Christ Jesus by the Holy Spirit when he subdues our corruptions, imparts to us grace, and leads us onward in the divine walk and life of faith. Christian men are not to be used for anything but God. They are a set-apart people; they are vessels of mercy, they are not for the devil's use, not for their own use, not for the world's use, but for their Master's use. He has made them on purpose to be used entirely, solely and wholly for Him. O Christian people, be holy, for Christ is holy. Do not pollute that holy Name wherewith you are named. Let your family life, your personal life, your business life, be as holy as Christ your Lord would have it to be. Shall saints be shams when sinners are so real?"*
>
> Charles Spurgeon

Bibliography

Holy Bible. New Kensington: Whitaker House, 2007. Print: King James Easy Reading

Ambrose, Isaac. Looking Unto Jesus. Pittsburgh: Luke Loomis & Co., 1882.
(Pg 374 "Christ crucified is the rarest piece of knowledge in the world.")

Pg 50
http://www.famousquotes.com/author/jonathan-edwards/
Jonathan Edwards - "Nothing sets a person so much out of the devils reach as humility."

Pg 147
http://www.goodreads.com/author/quotes/2876959.Charles_H_Spurgeon

"If sinners be damned, at least let them leap to Hell over our dead bodies. And if they perish, let them perish with our arms wrapped about their knees, imploring them to stay. If Hell must be filled, let it be filled in the teeth of our exertions, and let not one go unwarned and unprayed for."

Pg 147
http://www.goodreads.com/author/quotes/2876959.Charles_H_Spurgeon
"Let eloquence be flung to the dogs rather than souls be lost. What we want is to win souls. They are not won by flowery speeches."

Pg 148
http://www.goodreads.com/author/quotes/2876959.Charles_H_Spurgeon
"God has set apart His people from before the foundation of the world to be His chosen and peculiar inheritance. We are sanctified in Christ Jesus by the Holy Spirit when he subdues our corruptions, imparts to us grace, and leads us onward in the divine walk and life of faith. Christian men are not to be used for anything but God. They are a set-apart people; they are vessels of mercy, they are not for the devil's use, not for their own use, not for the world's use, but for their Master's use. He has made them on purpose to be used entirely, solely and wholly for Him. O Christian people, be holy, for Christ is holy. Do not pollute that holy Name wherewith you are named. Let your family life, your personal life, your business life, be as holy as Christ your Lord would have it to be. Shall saints be shams when sinners are so real?"

weseejesus
MINISTRIES

Adam LiVecchi, the leader of We See Jesus Ministries, lives by faith and has a heart to bring the Word of the Lord to the Body of Christ. His ministry is an itinerant ministry based in Northern NJ. As a result of the Lord's leading he has had the opportunity to minister internationally in Honduras, China, Mexico, Philippines, India, Peru, Dominican Republic, Brazil, Nicaragua, Haiti, Canada, Uruguay and all across the United States.

We See Jesus Ministries seeks to build the Kingdom of God through equipping the local church and delivering the Gospel message with signs and wonders following. Adam has the privilege of traveling with his beautiful wife, Sarah, and his brother, Aaron, who are both anointed musicians. Adam is also the co-leader of Voices in the Wilderness School of the Prophets rooted out of his local church in Woodland Park, NJ. Adam and Sarah LiVecchi look forward to building long lasting relationships that lead to sustainable change for the glory of King Jesus.

We See Jesus Ministries
31 Werneking Place
Little Ferry, NJ 07643
(973) 296-9050
WeSeeJesusMinistries.com
info@weseejesusministries.com

Voices in the Wilderness
School of the Prophets
86 Lackawana Ave Suite 243
Woodland Park, NJ 07424
VoicesintheWilderness.us
info@voicesinthewilderness.us

www.ingramcontent.com/pod-product-compliance
Lightning Source LLC
Chambersburg PA
CBHW052025290426
44112CB00014B/2389